WORLD
HISTORY SERIES ▪ ▪ ▪

The
Inca Empire

Titles in the World History Series

The Age of Augustus
The Age of Exploration
The Age of Feudalism
The Age of Napoleon
The Age of Pericles
The Alamo
America in the 1960s
The American Frontier
The American Revolution
Ancient Chinese Dynasties
Ancient Greece
The Ancient Near East
Architecture
Aztec Civilization
The Battle of the
 Little Bighorn
The Black Death
The Byzantine Empire
Caesar's Conquest of Gaul
The California Gold Rush
The Chinese Cultural
 Revolution
The Civil Rights Movement
The Collapse of the
 Roman Republic
Colonial America
The Conquest of Mexico
The Constitution and the Founding of
 America
The Crimean War
The Crusades
The Cuban Missile Crisis
The Cuban Revolution
The Early Middle Ages
Egypt of the Pharaohs
Elizabethan England
The End of the Cold War
The Enlightenment
The French and Indian War
The French Revolution
The Glorious Revolution
The Great Depression
Greek and Roman
 Mythology
Greek and Roman Science
Greek and Roman Sport
Greek and Roman Theater
The History of Rock & Roll

The History of Slavery
Hitler's Reich
The Hundred Years' War
The Inca Empire
The Industrial Revolution
The Inquisition
The Italian Renaissance
The Late Middle Ages
The Lewis and Clark
 Expedition
The Making of the Atom Bomb
The Mexican-American War
The Mexican Revolution
The Mexican War of
 Independence
Modern Japan
The Mongol Empire
The Persian Empire
Prohibition
The Punic Wars
The Reagan Years
The Reformation
The Relocation of the North
 American Indian
The Renaissance
The Rise and Fall of the
 Soviet Union
The Roaring Twenties
The Roman Empire
The Roman Republic
Roosevelt and the
 New Deal
The Russian Revolution
Russia of the Tsars
The Salem Witch Trials
The Scientific Revolution
The Spread of Islam
The Stone Age
The Titanic
Traditional Africa
Traditional Japan
The Travels of Marco Polo
Twentieth Century Science
The War of 1812
The Wars of the Roses
The Watts Riot
Women's Suffrage

WORLD
HISTORY SERIES

The
Inca Empire

by
Dennis Nishi

Lucent Books, P.O. Box 289011, San Diego, CA 92198-9011

Library of Congress Cataloging-in-Publication Data

Nishi, Dennis, 1967–
    The Inca empire / by Dennis Nishi.
        p.   cm. — (World history series)
    Includes bibliographical references and index.
    Summary: Discusses the Inca empire, including their traditional way of life, the reign of King Pachacuti, the last of the great kings, the Inca civil war and the end of the empire.
    ISBN 1-56006-538-9 (lib. : alk. paper)
    1. Incas—Juvenile literature. [1. Incas. 2. Indians of South America.] I. Title. II. Series.
F3429. N54 2000
985.019—dc21   99-045620
                                                                              CIP

Cover: Pizarro seizing the Inca of Peru by Sir John Everett Millais, 1845

Copyright 2000 by Lucent Books, Inc., P.O. Box 289011, San Diego, California 92198-9011

Printed in the U.S.A.

Contents

Foreword   6

Important Dates in the History of the Inca Empire   8

INTRODUCTION
The Land of the Incas   10

CHAPTER 1
Ten Thousand Years of Tradition   12

CHAPTER 2
The Incas   20

CHAPTER 3
Building an Empire   32

CHAPTER 4
Everyone Had a Place in Society   41

CHAPTER 5
The Last of the Great Kings   52

CHAPTER 6
A Historic Encounter   63

CHAPTER 7
Life Under Spanish Rule   74

Notes   83
For Further Reading   85
Works Consulted   86
Index   89
Picture Credits   95
About the Author   96

Foreword

Each year on the first day of school, nearly every history teacher faces the task of explaining why his or her students should study history. One logical answer to this question is that exploring what happened in our past explains how the things we often take for granted— our customs, ideas, and institutions— came to be. As statesman and historian Winston Churchill put it, "Every nation or group of nations has its own tale to tell. Knowledge of the trials and struggles is necessary to all who would comprehend the problems, perils, challenges, and opportunities which confront us today." Thus, a study of history puts modern ideas and institutions in perspective. For example, though the founders of the United States were talented and creative thinkers, they clearly did not invent the concept of democracy. Instead, they adapted some democratic ideas that had originated in ancient Greece and with which the Romans, the British, and others had experimented. An exploration of these cultures, then, reveals their very real connection to us through institutions that continue to shape our daily lives.

Another reason often given for studying history is the idea that lessons exist in the past from which contemporary societies can benefit and learn. This idea, although controversial, has always been an intriguing one for historians. Those who agree that society can benefit from the past often quote philosopher George Santayana's famous statement, "Those who cannot remember the past are condemned to repeat it." Historians who subscribe to Santayana's philosophy believe that, for example, studying the events that led up to the major world wars or other significant historical events would allow society to chart a different and more favorable course in the future.

Just as difficult as convincing students to realize the importance of studying history is the search for useful and interesting supplementary materials that present historical events in a context that can be easily understood. The volumes in Lucent Books' World History Series attempt to present a broad, balanced, and penetrating view of the march of history. Ancient Egypt's important wars and rulers, for example, are presented against the rich and colorful backdrop of Egyptian religious, social, and cultural developments. The series engages the reader by enhancing historical events with these cultural contexts. For example, in *Ancient Greece,* the text covers the role of women in that society. Slavery is discussed in *The Roman Empire,* as well as how slaves earned their freedom. The numerous and varied aspects of every-day life in these and other societies are explored in each volume of the series. Additionally, the series covers the major political, cultural, and philosophical ideas as the torch of civilization is passed from ancient Mesopotamia and Egypt, through Greece, Rome, medieval Europe, and other world cultures, to the modern day.

The material in the series is formatted in a thorough, precise, and organized manner. Each volume offers the reader a comprehensive and clearly written overview of an important historical event or period. The topic under discussion is placed in a broad, historical context. For example, *The Italian Renaissance* begins with a discussion of the High Middle Ages and the loss of central control that allowed certain Italian cities to develop artistically. The book ends by looking forward to the Reformation and interpreting the societal changes that grew out of the Renaissance. Thus, students are not only involved in an historical era, but also enveloped by the events leading up to that era and the events following it.

One important and unique feature in the World History Series is the primary and secondary source quotations that richly supplement each volume. These quotes are useful in a number of ways. First, they allow students access to sources they would not normally be exposed to because of the difficulty and obscurity of the original source. The quotations range from interesting anecdotes to farsighted cultural perspectives and are drawn from historical witnesses both past and present. Second, the quotes demonstrate how and where historians themselves derive their information on the past as they strive to reach a consensus on historical events. Lastly, all of the quotes are footnoted, familiarizing students with the citation process and allowing them to verify quotes and/or look up the original source if the quote piques their interest.

Finally, the books in the World History Series provide a detailed launching point for further research. Each book contains a bibliography specifically geared toward student research. A second, annotated bibliography introduces students to all the sources the author consulted when compiling the book. A chronology of important dates gives students an overview, at a glance, of the topic covered. Where applicable, a glossary of terms is included.

In short, the series is designed not only to acquaint readers with the basics of history, but also to make them aware that their lives are a part of an ongoing human saga. Perhaps they will then come to the same realization as famed historian Arnold Toynbee. In his monumental work, *A Study of History,* he wrote about becoming aware of history flowing through him in a mighty current, and of his own life "welling like a wave in the flow of this vast tide."

IMPORTANT DATES IN THE HISTORY OF THE INCA EMPIRE

1438
Pachacuti Inca Yupanqui defeats the Chanca and begins the Incas' golden age. The Inca capital is re-built from the ground up.

1493
Topa Inca dies and passes the royal fringe to his son Huayna Capac.

1435	1454	1473	1492	1511	1530

1463
An army under Pachacuti's son, Topa Inca Yupanqui, attacks and defeats the Chimu.

1471
Pachacuti dies and passes the royal fringe to Topa Inca Yupanqui.

1528
Spaniard Francisco Pizarro and his men visit the Inca city of Tumbez for the first time. Huayna Capac dies of smallpox, leaving his two sons to fight for control of the empire. A civil war begins.

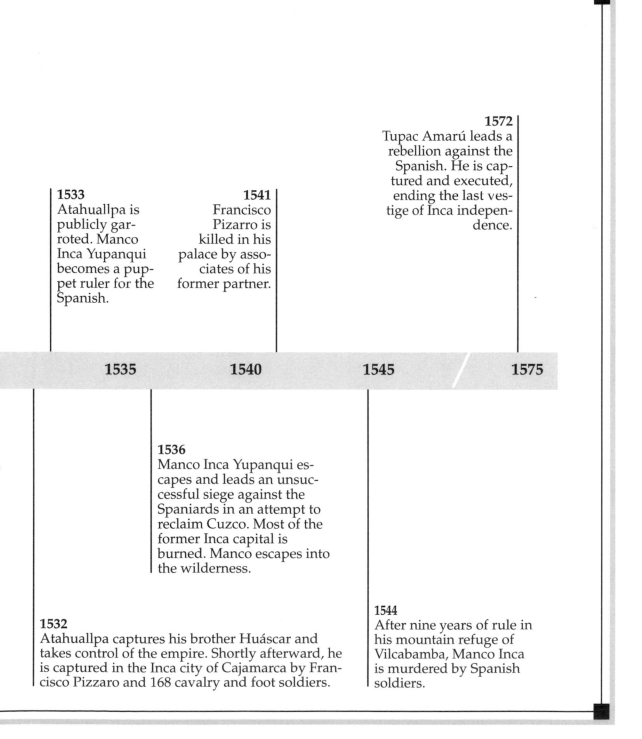

1533
Atahuallpa is publicly garroted. Manco Inca Yupanqui becomes a puppet ruler for the Spanish.

1541
Francisco Pizarro is killed in his palace by associates of his former partner.

1572
Tupac Amarú leads a rebellion against the Spanish. He is captured and executed, ending the last vestige of Inca independence.

1535 1540 1545 1575

1536
Manco Inca Yupanqui escapes and leads an unsuccessful siege against the Spaniards in an attempt to reclaim Cuzco. Most of the former Inca capital is burned. Manco escapes into the wilderness.

1544
After nine years of rule in his mountain refuge of Vilcabamba, Manco Inca is murdered by Spanish soldiers.

1532
Atahuallpa captures his brother Huáscar and takes control of the empire. Shortly afterward, he is captured in the Inca city of Cajamarca by Francisco Pizzaro and 168 cavalry and foot soldiers.

The Land of the Incas

The Incas called their empire Tahuantinsuyu, which means "the Land of Four Quarters." At its height, Tahuantinsuyu was the largest native empire in the Western Hemisphere, extending along the western coast of South America for over twenty-five hundred miles through dry coastal deserts, wind-swept plateaus and valleys, high snowcapped peaks, and mist-shrouded rain forests. The Inca Empire encompassed a land of geographical and climatic extremes. Writing in the sixteenth century, Spanish soldier and chronicler Pedro de Cieza de León considered many parts of the land to be "unfit for human habitation."[1] Such a view, however, did not take into account the Incas' resourcefulness in populating the land and making it prosperous.

The most distinguishing feature of the land of the Incas was the Andes mountain range. The highest mountains in the Americas, the Andes divided the Inca Empire into three unique geographical regions: the coastal deserts, the highlands, and the Amazon forests. The coastal deserts were, and still are, the driest deserts in the world. Despite the lack of rainfall, native peoples such as the Mochica and the Chimu thrived by tapping the rivers that flow westward from the Andes to the Pacific Ocean and using their water to irrigate the desert lands.

THE HIGHLANDS

Rising from the coastal deserts, the Andean highlands were home to the most powerful native empires. The Chimu, Tiwanaku, Huari, and Inca peoples had an advantage over the coastal peoples because they were closer to the sources of water. They could always defeat an enemy by merely blocking their water source from above.

The slopes of the Andean highlands were treacherously steep, but native farmers overcame this problem by cutting flat terraces into the hillsides.

Rising among the mountain peaks are punas, or high grassy plateaus. Punas are too high and too cold to be farmed, but the hardy grasses that grow there attract deer; vicuñas, which are related to llamas; and guanacos, which are related to camels. These animals provided both meat and wool to the native inhabitants.

On the eastern slope of the Andes, dense forests stretched down into the swampy Amazon basin. Heavy rainfall and numerous fast-rushing rivers made this lush zone impenetrable even to the highland peoples accustomed to a harsh climate. As a result, the fierce tribes living in the rain forests of the Amazon basin were among the few who could resist the rule of the Incas.

Andean farmers still use terraces to navigate the treacherous landscape of western South America.

MASTERS OF THE LAND

The ruggedness of the land provided a natural defense for small tribes of native peoples but also limited their growth and development. Natural resources were not plentiful, and trade between communities was difficult. Llamas were valuable for their fur and meat, but they could only carry about fifty pounds of weight. Therefore, the people of the Andes had to bear heavy loads on their own backs and travel on foot. Despite these disadvantages, the inhabitants of the Andean highlands met the challenges of the land. They built roads that stretched through all parts of the country. Even without the wheel or the horse, the Andean peoples were able to control thousands of square miles of territory. But it was a small highland tribe called the Inca that achieved what no other previous culture had. The Inca tribe brought the entire Andean region under one authority and one supreme god. In just a few hundred years, the Incas became the masters of the highlands, coasts, and valleys. They linked all of the different regions together to form the largest native empire in the Americas. Theirs was an achievement that still awes modern researchers.

1 Ten Thousand Years of Tradition

Modern-day scholars estimate that by the time of its defeat by the Spanish, the Inca Empire's population totaled as many as 6 million subjects. But the Inca Empire was not made up of all one people who spoke one language or worshiped the same god. The empire consisted of a multitude of different peoples and cultures that had been conquered or otherwise incorporated into it. The conquered were, however, allowed to keep many of their own languages and traditions. As author Ruth Karen writes, "The Incas governed all of these widely varied lands with finely calculated equity and an administrative machinery so superbly effective that it succeeded in welding the disparate peoples and civilizations that had grown, flourished and, in some instances, already decayed in these lands, into a single interdependent unit: a family of nations."[2]

The Incas' greatest strength was their ability to weave the best elements of past cultures into their own. They borrowed technology, art, and even gods from other cultures. When the Incas saw an idea or system that worked better than their own, they adopted the idea and improved on it where they could. For example, many of the Inca roads had already been in place

for thousands of years; the renowned Inca administrative system was adopted from the Chimu, who lived along the coast. The Incas had ten thousand years of rich tradition to draw upon, and they made the most of it.

THE CHAVÍN

Little is known of the most ancient cultures that rose and then disappeared from the Andean region. Most peoples were nomadic and widely scattered, and they left little record of their presence.

The first culture to leave behind physical evidence of itself is known as the Chavín, named for a single temple located in the Andean highlands. Little is known of the Chavín, but their buildings exhibit expert masonry skills and engineering. The temple known as Chavín de Huántar had elaborate air flow and drainage systems, for example.

THE WATER SOCIETIES

After the disappearance of the Chavín, the people of the region returned to a simpler

The Chavín was the first Andean culture to leave behind physical evidence of itself. This gargoyle on the wall at the temple Chavín de Huántar is an example of their expert masonry skills.

rior, every act is depicted in realistic detail. Moche pottery even records the drought and floods that were responsible for the fall of their empire.

FLOODS AND DROUGHTS

As the pottery shows, the strength of the desert kingdom was also its weakness. The Moche's extensive irrigation system made the dry sands of the valley floors fruitful, but the system was vulnerable to natural disasters. According to author James Richardson, "Alternating floods and droughts took a heavy toll on the abilities of the Moche to sustain their irrigation economy, and within the first 100

Many Moche pottery pieces depict the llama, which was valued by the Moche culture for its fur and meat and its ability to carry heavy loads.

lifestyle. However, they continued to develop important technologies such as irrigation, which allowed farmers to grow crops in areas where little rain fell. One group, the Moche of the northern coast, were the first culture in the region to depend completely on irrigation. They built a massive network of canals, an undertaking that required a high level of organization and planning. No single village could supply the manpower needed to construct public works projects on this scale, and the Moche by necessity became one of the first nation-states in the region.

Although the Moche left no written records, their daily life is recorded in their pottery. Every aspect of their lives has been illustrated on their pots and vases or in sculpture. From the toil of the lowliest laborer to the deeds of the bravest war-years of the Middle Horizon (A.D. 600 to 700), the Moche State collapsed, after more than 500 years of spectacular achievements in statecraft."[3]

THE HIGHLAND EMPIRE RISES TO POWER

As the balance of power shifted along the coasts and in the valleys, a new power arose in the Central Andes, this time in the highlands. The Tiwanaku culture, which flourished between A.D. 600 to 1000, became the first empire in the region. From their capital, located on the shore of Lake Titicaca, the Tiwanaku ruled over a region that encompassed the Titicaca basin and extended all the way to the Pacific Ocean.

The Tiwanaku capital, known by that same name, contained many buildings and pyramids constructed of enormous stone blocks. Tiwanaku masonry techniques, in fact, would be adopted by succeeding cultures. How the Tiwanaku managed construction of large stone buildings using tools made of bronze and stone is a source of wonder. For example, the blocks used in the Tiwanaku pyramid known as Pumapumku weighed up to one hundred tons each and were precisely cut and finished. Copper clamps, rather than mortar, were used to bind the stones together. As Pedro de Cieza de León writes, "I cannot understand or fathom what kind of instruments or tools were used to work them, for it is evident that before these huge stones were dressed and brought to perfection, they must have

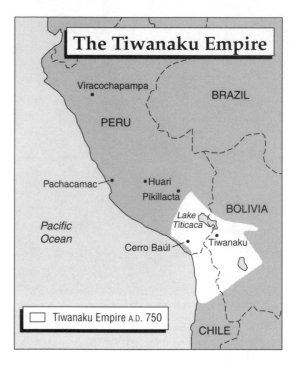

The Tiwanaku Empire

Viracochapampa

BRAZIL

PERU

Pachacamac

Huari
Pikillacta

BOLIVIA

Lake
Titicaca

Pacific
Ocean

Cerro Baúl

Tiwanaku

Tiwanaku Empire A.D. 750

CHILE

been much larger to have been left as we see them."[4]

Despite the sophistication of the Tiwanaku culture, these were not the people destined to rule an empire that stretched from the northern border of modern-day Ecuador south to the midsection of modern-day Chile.

THE CHILDREN OF THE SUN

In the Cuzco valley, north of Lake Titicaca and the Tiwanaku capital, a small highland tribe called the Inca emerged. It was one of many small tribes in the area, and little is known about it prior to its arrival in the region. What little information that is known has been handed down through the oral tradition in songs and stories. Over time the legends were undoubtedly embellished, so it is difficult to separate fact from fiction.

According to myth, four brothers and their four sisters emerged from caves in the mountains. The world was a dark place at the time and the people lived like animals. The eldest brother, named Manco Capac, was given a golden rod by the sun god with which to test the fertility of the soil. The eight siblings wandered the Andean highlands until they reached the Cuzco valley. There, Manco threw the golden rod and watched it sink deep into the earth. He turned to his sister, who was also his wife, and said, "Our father the Sun bids us remain in this valley and make it our dwelling place and home in fulfillment of his will. It is therefore right, queen and sister, that each of us should go out and call to-

Manco Capac holds the golden rod that, according to legend, was given to him by the sun god to test the fertility of the soil.

gether these people so as to instruct them and benefit them as our father the Sun has ordained."[5] Manco gathered the native people living in the wild and taught them how to build villages and harvest the many gifts of the earth. Manco's wife taught the women how to spin and weave cotton and make clothing. Together, they had many children and worked hard to build a good life. Before Manco died, he urged all of his sons and daughters to continue the work that he and his wife had started. They were, he said, the children of the sun and had a duty to civilize the people of the Andes through peaceful ways.

THE THIRTEEN INCA KINGS

Experts agree that the first Inca ruler, Manco Capac, was not a real person but a mythic figure created as a representation of early Inca culture and values. According to historian Alfred Métraux, "Manco Capac belongs to that vast pantheon of mythological persons placed by all Indian peoples at the dawn of their history. They are civilizers as well as being, by turn, gods, heroes and great ancestors."[6]

Other rulers succeeded Manco Capac, and each was credited in Inca lore with some great accomplishment. Manco Capac's eldest son, Sinchi Roca, was revered for having filled in the bogs around Cuzco and creating more farm land. Following Sinchi's death, Llonque Yupanqui became the third Inca ruler and was remembered for having created a class of provincial rulers called *curacas*. He also began the

INCA ORIGINS

"Some say that the settlers of this fourth part of the world came by land, spreading little by little from region to region; for this reason they suppose that America is connected with Asia somewhere. Others hold that they came by sea, possibly impelled by a storm, or on a planned voyage; and writers are not lacking who point out the nations and provinces from which they came. Some state that all these Indians spread out from one nation and these people came from Phoenicia and Carthage. Since they were very skillful in the art of navigation, these people came by their own design in a flotilla to this land, of which they had some information. Others say that these Indians descended from those Ten Tribes of the Hebrews, who were transported to a very remote region beyond the Euphrates River, where people had never lived before, and that from there, through Tartary, they came to North America, from whence they spread throughout the other part of the Indies. Still others say that they were descended from the inhabitants of that legendary island called Atlantis by Plato. Others are of the opinion that the natives of this New World are descendants of Spaniards, because they say that from them the Canary Islands were populated; and from these islands they came here. Others feel that the Romans populated this land at the time when their empire was largest and most powerful. To others it seems that the Indians descended from the Tartars and the Chinese."

practice of inspecting different parts of the realm under his control on a regular basis. The fourth ruler was Mayta Capac, who was renowned for his immense strength. According to legend, he leapt out of his mother's womb already endowed with great strength and a full set of teeth. Capac Yupanqui was the fifth ruler and the first one to venture outside of the Cuzco valley. Under his leadership, the Incas made their first conquests of coastal peoples. Capac Yupanqui's son Inca Roca was the sixth ruler and the first ruler to use *Inca* as a title meaning "head" or "leader." He was credited with starting a school for royal princes called the Yachahuasi. Yahuar Huacac became the seventh ruler, and although he is not credited with any great feats, his son would begin the Incas' rise to regional domination.

THE BEGINNING OF INCA HISTORY

Experts agree that the Incas' recorded history begins with the eighth Inca ruler, who adopted the name of the Incas' supreme god, Viracocha, before embarking on a campaign of conquest. Vira-

The eighth ruler of the Inca Empire adopted the name of the Incas' supreme god, Viracocha.

cocha's military prowess resulted in control by the Incas of 150,000 square miles of territory. Despite the fact that under his rule the Inca Empire had become a small but formidable state, powerful enemies threatened Cuzco from two directions. The Chanca loomed in the north and the Colla ranged to the south. The Chanca was an aggressive federation of different tribes that had launched a campaign of conquest in the region. After defeating the neighboring Quechua, the Chanca marched on the Incas. A now elderly Viracocha believed that his people could not withstand the Chanca, and he fled the capital with his son and heir to the throne, Prince Urco. The nobles of Cuzco (known as *orejones*) begged Prince Urco's younger brother, Prince Yupanqui, to defend them. The young prince dispatched messengers to offer Inca citizenship and land to anybody from neighboring tribes who would help defend Cuzco from the Chanca. Many people arrived to observe the battle but few offered to fight with the Incas, for fear that they would be caught on the wrong side at the end of the battle. Legend has it that at this point, Prince Yupanqui beckoned help from the earth. In response, legends say, the stones around the city turned into warriors and joined the Inca army.

MIGHTY KING CATACLYSM

Upon arrival in Cuzco, the Chanca leader, Hastu Huallaca, met with Prince Yupanqui to accept his surrender. When Yupanqui refused to surrender, the Chanca army

THE LARGE INLAND SEA

Following the Spanish conquest of the Incas, a soldier and historian named Pedro de Cieza de León traveled extensively through South America for seventeen years and wrote about the "strange and wonderful things that existed in the New World." In this excerpt from The Incas, *Cieza de León describes Lake Titicaca.*

"In the middle of the province there is a lake [Titicaca], the largest and widest that has been seen in most of these Indies. . . .

This lake is so large that it measures about eighty leagues in circumference, and so deep that Captain Juan Ladrillero told me that when he sailed it in his brigantines, the soundings in some places were seventy and eighty fathoms, and more, and in places less. In this and in the waves that arise when the wind blows it would seem to be an arm of the sea. What I mean to say is that all this water is locked in that lake, and nobody knows where its source is, for even though many rivers and brooks empty into it, it seems to me that they alone would not account for its volume, especially as the outlet from this lake drains into another smaller one known as Aulagas. . . .

The name of this great lake of the Colla is Titicaca from the temple that was built in the center of the lake. About this the natives had an idea that was pure superstition, and this is that they say their forebears asserted for a fact, like the other nonsense they tell, that for many days they were without light, and when they were all in darkness and gloom, there arose from this island of Titicaca the sun in all its splendor, for which reason they hold the island to be a hallowed spot, and the Incas built there the temple I have mentioned, which was one of the most venerated, in honor of their sun, bringing to it vestals and priests and great treasures."

An illustration of Lake Titicaca from Cieza de León's chronicles.

was called forward to charge the city. Author Loren McIntyre says that Prince Yupanqui leapt into the forefront of the battle with his generals to seize the Chanca *huaca* (stone idol). He writes, "The Incas captured the idol, striking terror into Chanca hearts. As soon as the spectators saw that the tide of the battle was turning in favor of the Incas, they poured from the hills and helped pursue the fleeing Chancas, stripping the wounded and dead of weapons and ornaments and turning the retreat into a rout."[7]

After the battle, Prince Yupanqui built a mausoleum outside the gates of the city. Inside the mausoleum, the bodies of the slain Chanca chieftains were stuffed with straw and ash and their skin was stretched to make drums out of their stomachs. When the wind blew, sticks placed in the hands of the lifeless Chanca would hollowly beat on their stomachs. The tomb was meant to show visitors to Cuzco the grisly fate that befell those who challenged the Inca.

Viracocha was not pleased with his son's victory over the Chanca. He realized that his position as ruler was being usurped and that Urco's legacy was being threatened. Viracocha sent Urco to kill Yupanqui, but Urco was unsuccessful and was killed in the attempt. After this incident, Urco's name was struck from the imperial record so that he would be forgotten. In a public ceremony, Viracocha was forced by the Inca nobles to give up his rule. The *orejones* then bestowed the red-tasseled royal fringe (the Incas' equivalent of a crown) upon Prince Yupanqui. The prince changed his name to Pachacuti, which, in the Quechuan tongue spoken by the Incas, meant "Cataclysm" or "He Who Transforms." It was an appropriate name for a ruler who would transform the Incas into an empire. Author John Hemming writes, "The great Inca ruler Pachacuti's victory in A.D. 1438 over the invading Chanca tribe in the hills above Cuzco propelled the Incas into their golden age, a century of unheralded territorial expansion and widening cultural hegemony."[8]

2 The Incas

After the defeat of the Chanca, Pachacuti wanted to completely rebuild Cuzco. The Inca capital had grown from the small village it once was into an unorganized jumble of adobe and thatch dwellings. It did not look like the religious and political power center of a growing empire. Pachacuti wanted the city to draw pilgrims from all over the empire and to awe those who visited it. Pachacuti had Cuzco abandoned and leveled; then, he laid out the new capital, using clay models to carefully plan the placement of lots for residents as well as for religious and public structures. Viewed from above, the outline of the city was shaped like a puma, an animal the Incas held sacred. Buildings would be arranged geometrically in quadrangular wards divided by narrow paved streets with curbs and a drainage system.

Pachacuti summoned thirty thousand men from all over the empire to work on the new capital. Hundreds of large storehouses filled with food such as maize, quinoa, and *chuño* (a spiced potato gruel); clothing; and other supplies were built on the surrounding hillsides to accomodate the needs of the workers during their stay. The men worked in shifts and were housed with others from the same region.

Pedro de Cieza de León writes that each group was designated a specific task: "Four thousand of them quarried and cut

Pachacuti, as drawn by Spanish chronicler Poma de Ayala in about 1620. Pachacuti proved to be one of the greatest military leaders that the Incas had ever known.

the stones; six thousand hauled them with great cables of leather and hemp; the others dug the ditch and laid the foundations, while still others cut poles and beams for the timbers."[9]

The inner city formed the puma's body. It was wedged between the Huatanay and Tullumayo Rivers, which had a tendency to flood their banks. To combat this problem, Pachacuti had stone-lined canals built to contain the waters. The royal palaces, administrative centers, temples, and other important buildings were built on the land reclaimed from the floodplain. Years later, Spanish chroniclers estimated that at the city's height there were over four thousand buildings in the inner city alone and another twenty thousand in the suburbs.

THE HEART OF CUZCO

At the heart of the new city was a central plaza, the Huacapata, which means "Holy Place" in Quechua. This was a place where the people of the city would make animal sacrifices to assure the next harvest, parade the mummies of their ancestors, and celebrate major military victories. Four roads converged onto the Huacapata from each corner of the empire. The arrangement was more than symbolic, writes author Ruth Karen:

Cuzco was, in fact, a political map of the empire. Each quarter represented its part of the empire, with vassal princes and administrators from their respective countries in permanent or temporary residence. A prince from Nazca, for example, in residence in

Cuzco, would live in the southwestern quarter of the city, while an administrator back from Quito to render report would be housed in the northeastern quarter.[10]

Cuzco's holiest sanctuary was built in the puma's tail and was called the Coricancha ("Enclosure of Gold"). It was a walled complex of individual temples, including Manco Capac's original Temple of the Sun. Each sanctuary was dedicated to one of five celestial gods in the Inca pantheon: the sun, the moon, the stars, the thunder, and the god who ruled all others, Viracocha. An image of each god resided in its own temple and was offered tribute daily. A separate sanctuary was used to store the *huacas* from conquered provinces. The Incas believed that these captive idols added to their power and allowed them to control the provinces from which the idols came.

Within each temple, gold was lavishly used for decoration. Gold was considered a sacred metal to the Incas, who considered it the sweat of the sun and the tears of the moon. As such, they used it to glorify their gods. As historian William H. Prescott writes,

Every part of the interior of the temple glowed with burnished plates and studs of the precious metal. The cornices which surrounded the walls of the sanctuary were of the same costly material; and a broad belt or frieze of gold, let into the stone-work, encompassed the whole exterior of the edifice. . . . The gardens, like those described belonging to the royal

THE CORICANCHA SURVIVES

The Coricancha was Cuzco's holiest shrine as well as an architectural marvel. After the Spanish conquest, Dominican friars built a church atop the Coricancha. In Loren McIntyre's book The Incredible Incas and Their Timeless Land, *the author writes of his visit to Cuzco shortly after a strong earthquake had toppled the Dominican church, uncovering a number of ancient Coricancha buildings.*

"I entered Cuzco not long after that instant clap of doomsday in 1950, picking my way among stone blocks flung from Inca walls like big black dice onto the cobbled streets. Surely this had been the sharpest quake since Pachacuti's day. Colonial buildings leaned and lurched; their second-story bedrooms—with front walls destroyed—were open to the streets and public squares as if they were theatrical sets. The Dominican church had caved in. 'Not the first time, but the worst,' a priest ruefully remarked. After tons of shattered masonry were cleared and layers of paint and plaster were scraped away to start the restoration of Santo Domingo, a wonderful thing emerged from all that havoc. Beneath the church several original Coricancha structures were found intact, their splendid walls undamaged by time or earthquake. Some of the finest Inca stonework had been protected by the act of building Santa Domingo church on top of it. Coricancha restoration proceeds, though hindered by lack of funds and the mass of the reconstructed Catholic church. The Dominican monks have moved out of their cells—the Inca shrines they occupied for 400 years—and opened them to tourists."

An original wall from the Coricancha, Cuzco's holiest shrine, serves as the foundation for a Spanish church.

palaces, sparkled with flowers of gold and silver, and various imitations of the vegetable kingdom. Animals, also, were to be found there—among which the llama, with its golden fleece, was most conspicuous—executed in the same style, and with a degree of skill which, in this instance, probably, did not surpass the excellence of the material.[11]

The temples' splendor was reserved for a privileged few to see. Although the Coricancha was meant to be a center for holy pilgrimage, commoners were denied entrance into the temples themselves. They had to make their token gestures to the sun god, Inti, along the curved wall outside. Only the emperor, who was the caretaker of the sun; the priests; and the chosen women who serviced the gods were allowed inside.

SERVICING INTI

The Coricancha was said to have a staff of four thousand. Among those who serviced the gods were the high priest and the chosen women, called *accla*. Selected for their unblemished beauty, the *accla* were young virgins who were to wed Inti. They spent their entire lives cooking; spinning thread; sewing beautiful tapestries; making *chicha*, a maize beer; and making daily offerings to the various gods in their shrines.

The *accla* lived in seclusion in a convent called the Accllahuaci, which means "the House of the Chosen Women." They were supervised and educated by nuns called *mamacunas*. The *mamacunas* also ensured the chastity of the *accla*, which was taken very seriously. Being unfaithful to Inti was considered a grave offense and was punishable by death. If an *accla* was caught being unfaithful, she was buried alive and her lover would be hanged. If the lover was married and had children, his family would also be killed and the village he lived in destroyed.

A HUB OF IMMENSE POWER

The Coricancha was significant as the religious center of the empire. Forty-one imaginary pathways, called *ceques*, radiated out from the Coricancha, pointing to 328 shrines located around the empire. The shrines were holy places mentioned in Inca mythology such as caves, hills, and battlefields.

But like the Huacapata, the Coricancha's significance was more than merely symbolic. One scholar observes, "Given the importance of irrigation, it is not coincidental that one-third of the ceque points comprised the major springs and water sources of the region."[12] Archaeologists believe that the Coricancha was the center of an enormous calendar, with each shrine representing a day in the Inca year.

A MONUMENT TO THEIR GREATNESS

The Incas' most impressive structure, the fortress of Sacsahuaman, formed the

The fortress of Sacsahuaman served many functions for the Incas: It protected them against enemies, sheltered the inhabitants, and stored food, clothing, and weapons.

puma's head. The stronghold sat on a hill-top protectively overlooking the city. It was an immense structure with three towers, zigzagging ramparts, and walls made of enormous stone blocks that weighed 90 to 120 tons each. As in all Inca stone structures, the blocks of Sacsahuaman were bound together without the use of mortar. But the Inca fortress took this technique a step further and interlocked the stones. A Spanish chronicler, Garcilaso de la Vega observed,

> Where a big rock had a concave side they would fit into it the convex part of another rock, as large or even larger, if they could find such, or similarly they would match the flat edge or slope of one rock with that of another. . . . This shows that the aim of the Indians was not to insert small stones into the walls, even to supply gaps in the larger ones, but to use only big rocks of remarkable size and to fit them together so that they served to strengthen one another and fill one another's gaps.

Garcilaso also writes that the fortress was as extensive below ground as it was above: "There were so many underground passages, large and small, twisting and turning in all directions, with so many doors, all of the same size, but some opening on one side and some on the other, that anyone entering the maze soon lost his way and was at a loss to find the way out."[13]

Sacsahuaman served several functions. Since Cuzco had no walls, Sacsahuaman was built to protect the city against siege and to shelter its inhabitants. Food, clothing, and weapons were stockpiled inside massive storerooms, and water was accessible from inside the fortress. Not only was Cuzco protected by its fortress, however: The Inca army was a formidable weapon that the emperor had at his disposal.

INCA WARFARE

Ever since the defeat of the Chanca, the Inca army had enjoyed a reputation for being divinely favored and unstoppable. This reputation alone was enough to take the fight out of many of the Incas' enemies. Chieftains from all over the surrounding territories came to Cuzco to voluntarily pledge their allegiance to the Incas, so a large part of the empire was gained without a struggle.

The Inca Empire also had an effective diplomatic strategy available. Before it sent its armies to battle an opponent, an emissary bearing gifts of gold and silver would seek an audience with the enemy *curacas*. The emissary would explain to the *curacas* the benefits of being incorporated into the empire. The *curacas* would also be told what happened to the enemies of the Inca Empire. If diplomacy failed, however, the army was sent in overwhelming numbers to intimidate the enemy. Just the sight and sound of a large column of Inca warriors marching toward them was sometimes enough to ensure a bloodless victory. When battles had to be fought, there were few opponents who could resist. The Inca army lived up to its reputation as being the mightiest in Peru.

THE MIGHTY INCA ARMY

At the peak of Pachacuti's reign, the Inca army was said to number two hundred thousand men. Ironically, most of them

Few opponents could resist the mighty Inca army, which was said to have numbered more than two hundred thousand men.

were not Inca by blood. Only the officers were full-blooded Incas chosen from the nobles of Cuzco. The majority of Inca soldiers were conscripted from conquered provinces. In fact, the first thing the Incas did after conquest was to draw warriors from the defeated enemy's army to help fight the next battle. Oftentimes a conquered people would immediately be pitted against other neighbors with whom they might already have a grudge. By this means, the new conscripts were given a stake in the conflict by allowing them to settle old scores.

Although the bulk of the Inca army was composed of commoners—mostly farmers—who were regularly drafted to fight, Inca warriors were more than draftees with weapons thrust into their hands. They were called on several times a month for regular drills. The emperor scheduled these drills and any military actions around important planting and harvest times, since to do otherwise would have created food shortages. While the men were away serving their time, other members of the community took care of their families and farming duties. After the campaign was completed, the army was disbanded and the warriors were allowed to return to their civilian lives.

The Inca army was one of the most well-equipped military forces in the Andes. Each soldier was issued quilted cotton armor and helmets made of woven cane. These garments provided effective protection against blunt weapons like clubs, maces, and stones from slings. Inca soldiers also carried shields covered with deerskin. For weapons, the Inca soldiers used spears, battle axes, pikes, clubs, lances, and maces. Since the Incas had not yet discovered iron, William H. Prescott writes, "their spears and arrows were tipped with copper, or more commonly, with bone, and the weapons of the Inca lords were frequently mounted with gold or silver."[14] Other weapons included bolas and slings, which could hurl stones. The weapons a soldier carried depended on which ones members of his particular tribe specialized in using.

As the time of battle neared, the Incas performed several rituals in preparation. One of these involved a sacrificial ceremony meant to weaken the enemy *huacas.* According to Ann Kendall, "The priests walked around a fire on which wild birds had been sacrificed. They carried stones on which snakes, toads, pumas and jaguars had been carved or painted, chanting: 'May it succeed' and 'May the idols of our enemies lose their strength'."[15] Inca priests then attempted to divine the outcome of the battle using the Calpa Ceremony, which involved sacrificing a llama and removing its lungs for inspection. Once removed, the priest blew into the lungs and watched the veins on the surface. If the lungs still quivered and swelled, the battle was foretold to have a good outcome.

THE TRIUMPHANT RETURN TO CUZCO

After a victory, the Incas celebrated with lavish feasts, drinking, and public humil-

INCA KNIGHTHOOD

In his Royal Commentaries of the Incas, *Garcilaso de la Vega describes the rigorous process that young Inca boys underwent to become warriors, or* huaracu.

"More or less every year or every other year, according to circumstances the young Incas underwent the military ordeal. . . . The candidates were required to observe a very strict fast for six days, receiving only a handful of raw sara (their corn) apiece and a jug of plain water, without anything else, either salt or uchu (which in Spain is called Indian peppers). . . . Such a rigorous fast was not usually permitted for more than three days but this period was doubled for the initiates undergoing their ordeal, in order to show if they were men enough to suffer any hunger or thirst to which they might be exposed in time of war. The fathers, brothers, and other close relatives of the candidates underwent a less rigorous, but none the less strictly observed, fast, praying their father the Sun to strengthen and encourage the youths so that they might come through the ordeal with honor. Anyone who showed weakness or distress or asked for more food was failed and eliminated from the test. . . . As a test they were made to run from the hill called Huanacauri, which they regarded as sacred, to the fortress of the city, which must be a distance of nearly a league and a half. . . . The next day they were divided into two equal bands. One group was bidden to remain in the fortress, while the other sallied forth, and they were required to fight one against the other, the second group to conquer the fort and the first defending it. . . . In such struggles the weapons were blunted so that they were less formidable than in real warfare; nevertheless there were severe casualties which were sometimes fatal, for the will to win excited them to the point of killing one another."

iation of the enemy and their gods. The celebration started with the Inca ruler making a grand entrance into the city on a golden throne borne high over his sub-

jects' heads. Prescott describes the scene: "The whole of its numerous population poured out to welcome him, dressed in the gay and picturesque costumes of the different provinces, with banners waving above their heads, and strewing branches and flowers along the path of the conqueror."[16] Prisoners from the conquered army were paraded through the narrow streets along with captured weapons, armor, and treasures for all the residents of Cuzco to see. The prisoners were then taken to the Huacapata and were forced to lie on the ground. The emperor then crossed the square, stepping on their bodies. The leaders of the vanquished foes suffered a fate that served as a warning to any future enemies. These men were sacrificed, and their skulls became cups from which to drink *chicha*. The rest of the prisoners, however, were returned to their homes unharmed.

THE CONQUERED WERE TREATED WELL

The Incas proved to be magnanimous victors. Once a battle was over, all hostilities were immediately ceased. The Incas did not plunder or destroy conquered cities and respected most native institutions. The conquered area became part of the Inca Empire and was entitled to all of the care and benefits bestowed on any other Inca province. As Spanish chronicler Pedro de Cieza de León relates,

> If there was a shortage of food in the province, he [the Inca emperor] ordered supplies brought in from other regions so that those newly won to his service would not find his rule and acquaintance irksome. . . . If in

any of these provinces there were no flocks, he instantly ordered that they be given thousands of head, ordering that they tend them well so they would multiply and supply them with wool for their clothing.[17]

Newly conquered people were even allowed to keep their cultural traditions and gods as long as they abided by the new Inca laws and customs.

The first thing that the Incas did after a conquest was to establish a garrison in the new province. The garrison protected the vulnerable cities from neighboring tribes who might seek to take advantage of a neighbor's weakened condition. The soldiers manning the garrison also acted as a police force for the conquered province. Officials called *quipucamayocs*, who acted as accountants, were then sent to the new province to observe and report on the living conditions of the people. The *quipucamayocs* used corded knots, called *quipus*, to take an inventory of llama herds, crops, mines, and anything else of value in the province. Their report was sent back to Cuzco, and the emperor and his advisers used it to calculate the amount of tribute to be paid by the emperor's new subjects. Tribute was always proportionate to what the people could produce and could be anything—from gold and silver to bushels of maize, wool, potatoes, human labor, and even children. If deceit was suspected, the offenders were severely punished. Huamán Poma, an Inca chieftain, describes the fate of *curacas* who cheated on their taxes: "Indians who committed offenses face the penalty of having a heavy stone dropped from a height on to their backs."[18]

INTEGRATION INTO INCA SOCIETY

After the tax rate was established for the conquered province, its residents were literally connected to the rest of the empire: A road was built to the new province. If any improvements or repairs needed to be made to buildings or other structures, engineers were sent. Irrigation canals were dug, and the hillsides were terraced to increase the amount of farmland. Sometimes, when locations were too inhospitable or too many buildings were unsalvageable, entire communities would be relocated to more arable land and an entirely new town would be built. Such improvements benefited both the victors and the vanquished. Smaller provinces typically lacked the resources and skilled workers to build large-scale public works themselves. And increasing the productivity of the land and the people, the Incas received more tribute in return.

To serve as the administrative center of the new territory, a new provincial capital would be built. The site of construction would be as close to the original capital as possible. A governor was personally appointed by the emperor to govern the province. "These governors had great authority and were empowered to raise armies and call up soldiers if there was some sudden disturbance or uprising, or if a foreign people came from anywhere to make war, and they were honored and favored by the ruler."[19] A temple devoted to the sun god was also built in the new capital to aid in the spread of the religion of the Incas.

THE TROUBLEMAKERS WERE MOVED

Some tribes did not adjust well to Inca life. As a last resort, the Incas relocated the

---

STONEWORK WITHOUT METAL TOOLS

In his book Peru Under the Incas, *author C. A. Burland describes the process the Incas used to work stone despite the lack of iron or steel tools the roadbuilding ordinarily requires.*

"It was a straightforward task to light a fire on a big rock and then douse the hot surface with water in order to start cracks. Then wooden wedges were inserted and soaked with water so that their expansion would rive the rock apart. When the process was simultaneously performed by hundreds of groups working on a stretch of road the speed of the clearance seemed quite incredible. The secret of road construction lay not so much in advanced technology as in superb organization."

troublesome communities to other parts of the empire and put a loyal community in its place. The relocation of these colonists, or *mitimaes,* was always done as gently as possible. They were moved to lands similar to the ones they came from and were relieved of their obligations to pay tribute until they could make the lands productive. For example, highlanders were moved into other highland regions, and coastal inhabitants were moved to another part of the coast. Prescott explains: "Even the habitual occupations were consulted, and the fisherman was settled in the neighborhood of the ocean or the great lakes, while such lands were assigned to the husbandman as were best adapted to the culture with which he was most familiar."[20] The communities that the *mitimaes* were moved into were selected for their loyalty to the Incas. The loyal residents helped ease the *mitimaes'* transition into their new homes and reported to the emperor any problems that might occur.

Transplanting entire communities this way not only brought security to the empire, but also helped indoctrinate different cultures in the Inca way of life without destroying native traditions. The *mitimaes* were moved as a whole, with all of their families and customs left intact. They were placed into regions and were influenced by Quechua-speaking Incas who worshiped the sun and practiced other Inca traditions. This practice allowed the Incas to bring the different peoples of the empire under a single religion, ruler, and tradition while using the minimum of force.

Capac Ñan: The Secret of Inca Success

The Inca could not have controlled their extensive empire without Capac Ñan, as the road that linked the provinces together was known. It was the secret of their success that they literally took with them to every conquest. In such a rugged land, keeping in regular contact with distant provinces would have been impossible otherwise. The road was a fourteen-thousand-mile system that linked every major city in the

Andes. It was designed to take the most appropriate route for whatever terrain it crossed. For example, if the road had to cross a desert, the route passed by available water sources. The road also took advantage of the Incas' engineering skills. If the road went up mountains, switchbacks would be cut into the hillsides to make ascent easier. Bridges were built over stream crossings, and suspension bridges were built over larger rivers. Some regions were so treacherous that the road could only make detours around them. Author Friedrich Katz notes, "Only by taking into account the extraordinarily difficult climatic and geographical considerations of the Andes region—the mountains, deserts, boglands and so on, is it possible to appreciate the achievement which this road system represents."[21]

The Incas also added *chasqui* posts and *tambos* every few miles along the road. *Chasqui* were runners who had been trained since a very young age to run at high altitudes. Their job was to relay messages from post to post. Thus, the *chasqui* allowed the emperor to stay in contact with his provincial governors. The *tambos* were storehouses for food, clothing, and weapons. If dissent was reported, the emperor could quickly send troops to quell any uprising. The *tambos* gave the Inca troops added mobility by allowing them to travel light. These storehouses also allowed troops to resupply on the move, which is why it was the road, *chasqui* posts, and *tambos* that were the first infrastructure to be built after a conquest. During times of drought or plague, the *tambos* helped communities in times of shortage.

Chapter

3 Building an Empire

Pachacuti proved to be one of the greatest military leaders that the Incas had ever known. He led the Inca army to victory in all four quarters of Tahuantinsuyu. But integrating all of the new conquests into the Inca way of life was a full-time job in itself. After a military campaign in which Pachacuti defeated the Colla in the Lake Titicaca basin, the Inca leader decided to stay in Cuzco and concentrate on reorganizing the empire. He gave command of the army to his brother, General Capac Yupanqui.

Capac continued the expansion of the empire by marching the Inca army north to attack the rival city of Huánuco. On this campaign, Capac was accompanied by a legion of Chanca warriors who had recently been added to the Inca ranks. The Chanca deserted before the army reached Huánuco. Capac pursued them for hundreds of miles without success. Rather than return in disgrace, the general sought to redeem himself by attacking another rival city, Cajamarca. He left a small garrison behind before returning to Cuzco with rich tributes for his brother. But Pachacuti was not pleased by his brother's hasty actions and ordered his execution. Cajamarca was allied with the Chimu Empire, and Pachacuti felt that the Incas were not

yet powerful enough to defeat the Chimu. Pachacuti sent his son and heir to the throne, Topa Inca Yupanqui, north to reinforce the garrison at Cajamarca.

Capac Yupanqui (pictured) was given command of the Inca army by his brother, Pachacuti. His military campaigns, though successful, were viewed as too aggressive by Pachacuti. Ultimately, Pachacuti ordered Capac's execution.

The Reign of Topa Inca Yupanqui

Topa quickly traveled north to reinforce the vulnerable outpost and found that the Chimu had not counterattacked as his father had feared they would. Topa began a new campaign and advanced north, building his army with every new conquest. He pushed the Inca frontier all the way to Quito, which in modern times is the capital of Ecuador, before turning south to attack the coastal Chimu. The Chimu had already prepared their capital, Chan Chan, for an Inca siege, but they never expected an assault by the Incas from the north. After a series of bloody campaigns, Topa defeated the Chimu by threatening to cut off their water supply.

Victory over the Chimu was one of the Incas' most important conquests. But Topa decided not to stop with the Chimu. He took the army south and conquered the entire southern coast. Upon the death of Pachacuti, Topa Inca Yupanqui became the tenth ruler of the Inca Empire.

Putting All of the Numbers Together

Between them, Pachacuti and Topa were responsible for the greatest expansion of the empire. But empire building required more than strong military leadership. Pachacuti and Topa distinguished themselves as great statesmen as well. They developed an efficient administrative system that was able to monitor and regulate the many provinces brought into the Inca Em-

The tenth ruler of the Inca Empire, Topa Inca Yupanqui. Topa and his father, Pachacuti, were responsible for the greatest expansion of the empire.

pire. Considering how fast the empire grew and the amount of record keeping required, this was an impressive feat, especially considering that the Inca culture never developed a written language.

Despite the lack of a written language, the Incas managed to keep detailed records, and the secret to this record keeping was the *quipu*. The *quipu* was a two-foot-long cord with wool threads hanging from it like fringe. The threads were of different colors and featured knots tied in different places. Experts believe that the knots were thought to represent different decimal values. One researcher believes that the colors also had a literal representation, which allowed the Incas to keep track of events: "The colors denoted sensible objects; as, for instance, white represented silver, and yellow, gold. They sometimes also stood for abstract ideas. Thus, white signified peace, and red, war."[22] Inca accountants, called *quipucamayocs*, used the *quipu* to tally everything

Although the Incas never developed a written language, the quipu—*a two-foot-long counting device with wool threads—made it possible for the empire to keep detailed records.*

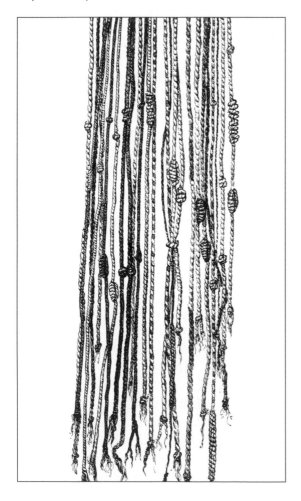

from *tambo* inventories to the number of new babies born in a province and the amount of taxes owed. There was a *quipucamayoc* in every capital, and he regularly sent reports to the imperial capital of Cuzco. Beyond their skill and resourcefulness at record keeping, however, the Incas proved to be masters at organizing.

ORDERS OF TEN

With a population of millions, administrators at every level had to make certain that everyone was contributing their share of tribute to the state. To aid in this process, the taxpayers in every province of the empire were divided into easily manageable groups of ten. Each group had its own leader. The foundation of the system began with the taxpayer, or the head of the family. Ten taxpayers were accountable to a foreman. The foreman was accountable to someone else, to whom five foremen reported. The hierarchy continued in an unbroken line to the provincial governor, or *tocricoc apu*, who was near the top of the scale. He controlled four groups of ten thousand taxpayers and reported to one of four *apus*, who each administrated one of four regions of the empire. The regional *apu* was only accountable to the emperor.

All of the administrators below the *apu* were appointed by their superiors. The *apu* and the provincial governors were appointed by the emperor himself. Only the members of the nobility in Cuzco received appointments to these high positions, which, according to author Ruth Karen, were based on merit: "They were exacting

The Imperial Census

Much of the Incas' success can be attributed to their strong organizational abilities, and key to their organizing efforts was an accurate census. Without a regular census, the Incas could not possibly control their vast empire. In his history of the Inca Empire, Spanish chronicler Pedro de Cieza de León describes how the Incas used quipus *to keep track of their people.*

"The Orejones of Cuzco who supplied me with information are in agreement that in olden times, in the days of the Lord-Incas, all the villages and provinces of Peru were notified that a report should be given to the rulers and their representatives each year of the men and women who had died, and all who had been born, for this was necessary for the levying of the tributes as well as to know how many were available for war and those who could assume the defense of the villages. This was an easy matter, for each province at the end of the year had a list by the knots of the quipus of all the people who had died there during the year, as well as of those who had been born. At the beginning of the new year they came to Cuzco, bringing their quipus, which told how many births there had been during the year, and how many deaths. This was reported with all truth and accuracy, without any fraud or deceit. In this way the Inca and the governors knew which of the Indians were poor, the women who had been widowed, whether they were able to pay their taxes, and how many men they could count on in the event of war."

positions because the Inca system demanded taut competence at every level of administration and each administrator was held personally responsible for the performance and the well-being of each individual under his jurisdiction."[23]

The *Ayllu*

Administratively, the entire Inca Empire was divided into tens; socially, it was divided into clans called *ayllus*. Each *ayllu* had a specific role and duty to fulfill in Inca society, and its members worked together to achieve these common goals. The commoner, the noble, and even the emperor and his family were born into an *ayllu*, each of which had a common ancestor who was worshiped. Author Michael E. Moseley notes, "Ayllus were often named after their founders, who were heroic figures, if not mythical ones, and could turn into stone or some special object. They secured lands for their people, established codes of behavior, and were models for proper life."[24]

Members of the *ayllu* were responsible for supporting their common ancestor with regular offerings. The remains, which had been mummified, were venerated and brought out during special events. This Inca tradition of ancestor worship had been instituted by Pachacuti and was especially costly for the royal family. A commoner's obligation to an ancestor ended after the deceased's grandchildren died; members of the royal family, however, serviced their ancestors and their lands in perpetuity. A permanent staff of servants served their dead master's mummy and his earthly possessions in case the soul returned to Earth. The tradition turned a huge amount of valuable land throughout the Inca Empire into a memorial for the Incas' dead. More-

The Inca tradition of ancestor worship involved preserving the dead through mummification. This eleventh- or twelfth-century gold mummy mask was found in an Inca tomb.

over, the spoils that were accumulated over a lifetime of conquests were not inherited by the succeeding prince, which forced each new ruler to undertake conquests to build his own fortune.

THE RELIGIOUS CASTE

Within this strictly ordered society, the religious caste was no different from the rest of the empire in its organization. This caste was a large institution and was supported by the labors of the taxpayer. Like the empire it served, the religious caste was divided into hierarchical groups that were in turn led by the *uillac uma*, or high priest, and his council of ten *hatun uillca*, or bishops.

At the bottom of the hierarchy were the *yana uillca*, who were regular priests chosen from families of the *curacas*. These priests were the workhorses of the religious caste. They served the sun temples built throughout the empire and had many duties, including listening to the confessions of the worshipers and acting as diviners to predict the future. They were the *amautas* (teachers) who were responsible for educating members of the royalty and nobility. They also participated in the regular festivals throughout the course of the year. Since the religious calendar was tied into cycles of Inca agriculture, the *yana uillca* performed the rituals that celebrated animal fertility or marked the beginning of planting or harvest seasons.

The *hatun uillca* each directed one of the empire's ten religious districts. They were nobles of royal blood who were ap-

Burial Customs

When somebody died in Inca society, they were buried with food and clothing as well as other material goods and even servants and companions. The Incas believed in taking the rich comforts of the world with them into the afterlife. In his Letter to a King, *Huamán Poma describes the funerary process of the Incas.*

"Before their burial the Incas were embalmed and care was taken to avoid any damage to the body. The eyes and face were arranged to look exactly as they had done in life. The dead rulers were then dressed in their richest clothing. . . . It was the custom to bury the Incas with a quantity of gold and silverware and with the pages, servants and women who had been their favourite companions in life. The best loved of the women was designated as Queen for this purpose and was killed with the others before burial. . . .

The bodies were kept on show for a full month while in the whole country there was a period of mourning celebrated not only with tears but with music, singing and dancing. At the end of this time the bodies were carried to the vault called a pucullo. The solemn ceremonies, with presents of gold and silver and other valuables, continued up to the moment of burial."

pointed by the *uillac uma*. The *uillac uma* resided at the top of the order. He was second only to the emperor in power and appointed by the emperor, who typically chose a brother or uncle for the job, which he held for life.

The *uillac uma* resided in Cuzco and maintained the highest shrine of the land, the Coricancha. From Cuzco, he governed the entire religious caste with the help of the *hatun uillca*. The *uillac uma* was the "supreme judge and arbiter in all religious questions and causes relating to the temples"[25] and was responsible for appointing the officials for the temples. The *uillac uma*

also personally performed important sacrifices.

A Gesture of Faith

Every major event in the Inca Empire was preceded by a sacrifice that was meant to earn the favor of the gods. Llamas, lambs, and guinea pigs were the most common subjects of sacrifice. Each god required its own specific ritual and animal. White llamas, for example, were always sacrificed in any ceremony for the sun god, and a brown llama was always sacrificed for Viracocha.

THE DISCOVERY OF JUANITA

The 1995 discovery of the well-preserved remains of an Indian child on Mount Ampato is giving experts an insightful peek into Inca sacrificial rituals. Affectionately named Juanita by archaeologists, the young girl was estimated to have died in the late 1400s. This article was reported for Newsday *in 1996 by special correspondent John Otis.*

"An eruption by a neighboring volcano had melted Mount Ampato's snowcap, exposing Juanita's grave, but not yet causing the corpse to melt. . . . The site contained a treasure of gold, silver and bronze statuettes, ceramics and eating utensils and clothing. Never before have archaeologists found such a complete set of relics and remains at a ceremonial Inca site. . . . The artifacts and X-rays offer clues about what happened to Juanita and the other mummies [found in a second expedition], who were between the ages of 12 and 15 at their death. One of the key mysteries is whether they were killed and later carried to the top of Mount Ampato, or put to death at the summit. . . . Researchers are already theorizing that vomit stains found on her clothes probably indicate that she was given 'chicha,' an alcoholic beverage made of fermented corn, to make her drowsy, and that she died of exposure. X-rays of Juanita show no broken bones, and there are no external signs of a violent death. They've carefully begun peeling back some of Juanita's outer clothing, scientists said, and soon hope to begin studying unfragmented DNA from her body in an effort to determine the state of Juanita's health, and to make genetic comparisons between the Incas and modern-day Peruvians."

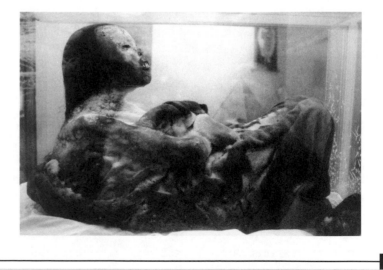

Juanita, displayed in a Peruvian museum.

Afterward, the blood of the animal was smeared onto the appropriate *huaca*.

Only rarely was the blood of a human required by the Inca gods. When the empire was besieged by drought or pestilence, however, a child would be sacrificed in a ceremony called *capaccocha*.

The child chosen for sacrifice was usually the most beautiful son or daughter of the emperor himself; this was the greatest sacrifice an Inca ruler could make for his people. A feast would be given to honor the child, followed by a solemn march up the mountain where the sacrificial platform and burial tomb were located. The child would be given *chicha* to dull his or her senses and was then wrapped in a shroud and placed inside the tomb. Sacred objects such as golden llamas would be placed inside as well, to accompany the child to the afterlife. Tribute would be regularly left on the platform after the child's death.

Until recent times, very little was known about *capaccocha* except what was written by Spanish chroniclers. The discovery of frozen mummies high in the Andes has helped give experts some insights into the Inca rite and has also posed new questions. One unanswered question is whether the child was killed before he or she was placed in the tomb. Many of the mummies show evidence of skull fractures, which causes experts to speculate that a blow to the head might have been administered to hasten death and prevent suffering.

THE EMPIRE HAD MANY GODS

Despite the importance of religion in Inca society, the Incas did not stop those they conquered from worshiping the gods they had always worshiped. In fact, the Incas occasionally incorporated gods from other cultures into their own pantheon. As a result, the Inca religion was a large melting pot of beliefs. Spanish chronicler Garcilaso de la Vega noted, for example, that the Peruvians seemed to worship a large number of animals and inanimate objects:

> They worshipped grasses, plants, flowers, trees of all kinds, high hills, great rocks. . . . They also worshipped other animals for their cunning, such as the fox and the monkeys. They worshipped the dog for its faithfulness and nobility, the wild cat for its quickness. . . . Others adored the earth and called it "mother," because it gave them its fruits. . . . The coastal Indians, in addition to an infinity of other gods they had even including those already mentioned, generally worshipped the sea, which they called Mamacocha, or "Mother Sea," implying that it was like a mother to them in sustaining them with its fish.[26]

Within the world they could see, the Incas considered the sun to be the supreme god. The empire's subjects were also required to revere Inti over all of their own gods and to worship him in the sun temples that were built in every province. For the Incas, the sun represented everything good that they depended on for their survival. The Inca people were farmers first and foremost, and the sun brought warmth and light to nurture crops. Moreover, its absence brought darkness, cold, and death.

The One God

More powerful even than the god of the sun, ruling over things seen and unseen, was Viracocha, the supreme god of beginnings. Viracocha was incoporated into the Inca pantheon later, and placed above Inti. What made Viracocha different from the other gods the Incas worshiped was his abstract nature. Viracocha was not represented in nature or anywhere else in the world, but he resided invisibly in the heavens. The Incas believed that Viracocha was the creator of all things, including the sun, moon, and stars. Viracocha, the Incas believed, walked on Earth and brought civilization to the people.

Garcilaso de la Vega noted that the Incas also believed in an afterlife, which included a heaven (Hanan Pachua) and a hell (Uca Pacha). The Incas believed that the quality of an individual's life determined the quality of his or her afterlife. Virtuous souls went to Hanan Pachua, which was a world of comfort and ease. Evil souls went to Uca Pacha, which was a world full of sickness, pain, and unrelenting needs that could never be sated. The Inca faithful confessed wrongdoings to a priest, who then meted out penance that must be met before a pardon could be granted. Author George Bankes notes that confessions had to be complete and accurate. "If the would-be confessor was found to be telling lies or half-truths a stone would be dropped on his back."[27]

Chapter

4 Everyone Had a Place in Society

The subjects of the Inca Empire were given everything they needed to live productive lives. They were protected and given homes and land for farming, food to eat, clothing to wear and even a bride or groom to marry. When droughts or floods destroyed crops and livestock, food and clothing were brought from other parts of the empire for distribution to those in need. If a neighboring tribe threatened to invade, the Inca army was sent to repel the attack. All that was asked in return was a hard day's work from each man and woman and a share of the crop harvests or whatever other service each person provided to the state.

All of this security came at a price, however. There was very little individual freedom in Inca society. Every aspect of a person's life from birth to death was controlled by the state. According to author John Hemming,

> The entire lifetimes of both men and women were divided into discrete age groups, with specific tasks allotted to each. Children, for instance, were put to tending flocks of llamas, while adolescents performed agricultural tasks or felled wild birds with their slings.

. . . There was also complete control of movement, language and even dress of the empire's citizens.[28]

There was no social mobility in Inca society. It was caste oriented, which meant that people stayed in the social group into which they had been born. People born into a farming *ayllu*, for example, usually died farmers and reared children who also became farmers. On rare occasions, commoners who distinguished themselves in some way could rise above their class. For instance, exceptional heroism in battle could earn a commoner a position within the government and even honorary rank among the nobility. But even those bestowed nobility would always hold a lower rank than a noble who was born into his or her position.

COMMONERS DID ALL OF THE WORK

Although commoners held the lowest positions in Inca society, the power of the empire came from their labor. Most commoners were farmers who were expected to grow enough food to support not only themselves but also to provide a share for the state. According to historian Ruth Karen, "A second part was set aside for the 'sun,' which meant the priesthood and all ritual and ceremonial purposes. The third part was allocated to the Inca. This included not only the ruler and his family but all segments of society that worked directly for the state such as military, educators, court attendants of a wide range and variety, and craftsmen."[29]

Commoners had many other obligations in Inca society. Before working on their own lands, they were required to maintain the lands of the sick, disabled, and widowed in the community. They were also required to work on the lands of those who had been conscripted to work on some public works project. At any time, the commoner could be summoned to fight in the army; help build bridges, roads, and canals; or farm the lands of imperial officials or the emperor himself. When the commoner was called to duty, he could always be assured that his family and land would be taken care of by

EVEN THE *SAPA* INCA LIKED TO GAMBLE

The Incas were not all work, though many Inca games and sports had the purpose of honing physical skills for future battle. In her book Everyday Life of the Incas, *Ann Kendall describes the gambling games enjoyed by the Incas.*

"There were a number of games in which dice were used. The dice, Picaqana, were marked with one to five points and may have been made of ceramic or wood. Hard, inedible chuy beans of different colours with comic names were used, both for keeping scores and for playing games. In one such game, movements of the beans were controlled by the throw of the dice. The Incas gambled on these games for amusement, exchanging clothes, and animals as part of the fun. The tenth [*sapa*, or emperor] Inca, Topa Inca Yupanqui, seems to have been something of a gambler. On one occasion he accepted a challenge from his favourite son, to play a dice throwing game called ayllos, introduced from the [Colla], and he agreed to give his son one of his provinces if he should win. The game was watched by worried spectators who feared the Inca's behaviors if he should lose. However, the Inca ruler did lose and eventually he gave his son the governorship of the province of his choice—Urcosuyu. Henceforth those who inhabited this province were called the Aylluscas in memory of the story."

this system of compulsory service, known as the *mita*.

IN THE EMPLOY OF THE KING

Compared to the commoner, the artisans in Inca society had an easy life. Although not nobles themselves, artisans and their families were supported by the *orejones* and the royal court. They were exempt from paying tribute or working on public works projects. They were given everything they needed to live and all of the tools and materials they needed for their work. All that was required of them was to create luxury goods for the state. Such goods could be anything from the smallest military medal to the life-size golden image of Inti housed in the Coricancha. The best artisans in the Andes were brought from their native lands to work in Cuzco.

Metalsmiths were held in especially high esteem. Gold, before it was worked, was worthless, but after it was molded into some object, it became holy. The Chimu, in particular, were known throughout the Andes for their finely crafted jewelry and crafts. After Topa Inca Yupanqui conquered the Chimu capital of Chan Chan, Chimu metalsmiths were immediately sent back to Cuzco to teach their craft to the Incas. According to author Ann Kendall, "The Chimu and the Inca had a wider knowledge of different processes in metal technology than any other people in Pre-Columbian America. The techniques included many of those used today: hammering, annealing [heating and cooling], casting in open and closed moulds, plat-

Most tools and luxury goods were created from metal by the finest artisans in the Andes.

ing."[30] Although the conservative Incas considered the Chimu style to be decadent and made the artists conform to an Inca style, they appreciated fine craftsmanship in any form.

THE OREJONES

Above the artisans in Inca society were the nobles, of whom there were two types: the nobles of royal blood and those known as "Inca by Privilege." The nobles enjoyed many privileges in Inca society that commoners were denied, including generous land grants, fine clothing, concubines, and servants. The nobles benefited from the labors of the artisans and were entitled to wear the golden earplugs that led early Spanish observers to refer to them as *orejones*.

The nobles of royal blood were descendants of past Inca rulers. Positions in the highest levels of the Inca government, the priesthood, and the army were reserved for these well-born individuals. They were exempt from paying tribute and working the *mita*. They even received favored treatment in the justice system. If nobles were found guilty of a crime, they typically received a more lenient punishment, if any, than a commoner who committed the same crime. As historian William H. Prescott explains, "The laws, severe in their general tenor, seemed not to have been framed with reference to them [nobles]; and the people, investing the whole order with a portion of the sacred character which belonged to the sovereign, held that an Inca noble was incapable of crime."[31]

This Inca kero, or goblet, was used during religious rituals. This example represents a stylized "big ear," or orejone—*a nobleman who wore golden earplugs.*

Unlike their high-born counterparts, those who were "Inca by Privilege" were not Inca by birth but rather chieftains of conquered provinces who cooperated with the new government and became honorary *curacas*. Since there were not enough royal-blood nobles to occupy every post in the expanding empire, nobility was bestowed to those *curacas* who exhibited exceptional administrative skills. After the initial appointment, the position became a hereditary title. The "Inca by Privilege" were considered of lower social standing than royal-blood nobles. They served in lower positions and were even made to dress in a way that distinguished them from the royal-blood nobles.

AN ACADEMY FOR PRINCES AND NOBLEMEN

To be born a noble in Inca society was not enough. Nobles required schooling in the duties they were expected to fulfill. Every young noble, whether born or appointed into the elite class, was obligated to attend the university in Cuzco called the Yachahuasi. For the royal-blood Incas, the school prepared them for a career within the government. For the sons of *curacas* from conquered lands, it was a way to indoctrinate them in the ways of the Incas. As it happened, the practice also served to provide the Incas with hostages, thereby ensuring the continued loyalty of these non-Inca officials.

Instruction at the Yachahuasi lasted four years and included courses ranging from Inca statecraft and the use of the *quipu* to history, philosophy, astronomy, military tactics, and the religion of the empire. For students unfamiliar with the tongue, Quechua was taught first, since it was the official state language. The Incas did not force students to abandon their native tongues but did insist that they learn Quechua so that once they began to work they could communicate with the rest of the empire. Students were also required to teach Quechua to their families, children, and the general population in their native provinces. Through this standardization of the language, the Incas unified their diverse empire.

Students at the Yachahuasi also received rigorous physical training, which included an annual survival competition that functioned as one of the final exams. Teams of students were sent into the wilderness unarmed and without food. They were expected to use the skills they learned at the university to find food, make weapons, and survive long enough to pass the test.

THE *SAPA* INCA SAT HIGH

The emperor, or *sapa* Inca ("unique" Inca) enjoyed complete power at the top of Inca society. He was the head of the government and created laws, appointed the highest officials in the empire, and levied taxes. He was also the head of the army and could summon conscripts from all four quarters, send them anywhere in the empire, and personally lead them into battle. He was the head of the priesthood and a deity himself. Historian William H.

Prescott notes, "He was, in short, in the well-known phrase of the European despot, 'himself the state.'"[32]

But the emperor was more than just a leader. The *sapa* Inca was worshiped as divine by his subjects. He was the son of the sun and was thus the closest Inca on Earth to Inti. Even the nobility, who claimed common royal bloodlines, were required to appear before the emperor with bare feet, their eyes downcast and a burden balanced on their shoulders. Only the highest-ranking members of the nobility were even allowed to sit in the emperor's presence. But the Inca did not always keep his distance from his subjects. Every few years the emperor traveled among his people and personally inspected his provinces. He traveled on a golden litter that was borne by a chosen few royal bearers and spoke to the commoners. He listened to their problems and took note of any suggestions for changes or improvements.

The royal court of the *sapa* Inca included his *coya* ("empress"), who was also his eldest full-blooded sister. Marriage to such a close family member was a tradition that Inca rulers followed to keep the royal bloodlines pure. Although the emperor's wife was a close relative, Inca emperors had large harems of concubines as well. Emperor Huayna Capac, for example, was known to have accumulated seven hundred women.

DAILY LIFE OF THE INCAS

In contrast to the lifestyles of the emperor and the nobles, the typical Inca citizen lived in very austere surroundings. Homes were often single-room dwellings with thatched roofs, packed dirt floors, and no windows. They slept on reed mats and blankets; furniture might consist of a stool or bench for seating. Baskets and pots were used to store food and weaving materials, and a small clay stove was used for cooking and heating.

When the Incas awoke in the morning, they ate small breakfasts and nothing else until dinner. Dinner was considered the main meal of the day and was not eaten before sundown. The staples of the Inca

Incas dig and harvest potatoes. Because meat was scarce, maize, potatoes, and quinoa were staples of the Inca diet.

diet were maize, potatoes, and quinoa. These were combined with different types of beans to make stews and soups. Meat was scarce and was thus not an important part of the Incas' diet. In fact, most meat was eaten during festivals and special ceremonies if at all.

During festivals, the entire community would eat in the home of the local *curaca*. For such community meals, everyone brought food and drink to be shared in a potluck. *Chicha* was consumed in great quantities during these festivals. Historian Bernabe Cobo remarks, "For this reason, they make it often and in batches of four to six arrobas [sixteen to twenty-four gallons] at a time. Considering the large amounts they drink, this much lasts a man no more than a week, more or less."[33]

Individuality was discouraged in Inca society, and everybody, regardless of class, was required to dress in a style typical of their native region. Clothing, then, functioned as a kind of uniform that made it easy to tell which class someone belonged to and where he or she came from.

Regardless of a person's class, Inca clothing was typically made of warm materials such as wool because of the cool temperatures typical of the highlands. Commoners wore very simple garments that they made themselves out of undyed materials of a rough quality. The nobility and the royal family, on the other hand, wore clothing made of the finest materials, such as vicuña wool, which was imprinted with brightly colored patterns. Women wore long dresses that were secured with sashes or belts and threw cloaks around their shoulders that were

The tunic of an Inca nobleman. Made of golden plaques sewn onto fabric, this piece probably came from a looted tomb.

fastened with silver or bronze pins. Men wore tunics that fell above the knee and loincloths underneath them.

A Husband and Wife Were Chosen for Each Other

No aspect of Inca life was free of regimentation, and this included decisions regarding finding a mate. Regardless of class or trade, everybody in Inca society was required to marry. Not only was remaining single not an option, but for commoners there was typically little choice of whom they would marry. Like everything else in the empire, marriage was a state matter that was arranged by an administrator. Unmarried men and women of the same age were simply paired off by the *curacas*. Chances were

good, however, that the bride and groom would at least know each other, since all couples were required to marry within the same *ayllu*. Moreover, it was unheard of for two people from different regions of the empire to marry.

The selected couples would be married in a communal ceremony held once a year. It was performed by the *curacas* or in Cuzco by the *sapa* Inca himself. A celebration would be held afterward with feasts, singing, and dancing. Once married, a man was given a year to establish a life for himself, his wife, and his future children. The husband built a house and cultivated a small plot of land granted to the newlyweds by the state. The wife supported her husband by performing domestic duties like making the family's clothing, cooking, and taking care of children. Women were also supplied with wool to make clothing for the state; every spare moment was spent weaving.

ADDING TO THE WORKFORCE

The Incas saw children as future additions to the workforce and as future taxpayers. For this reason, newly married couples were encouraged to have children as soon as possible. But everyone's labor was needed, so when a woman became pregnant, she continued to work for as long as she was able and immediately returned to work after giving birth. The one exception was if the woman gave birth to twins. Despite the value that the Incas placed on children, the birth of twins was considered a bad omen that required special rituals and fasting.

Once children were born, it was customary among the Incas not to pamper them in any way. Coddling was thought by the Incas to make children weak and prone to cry, so mothers seldom held their babies. Instead, they kept babies in cradles at all times and even washed and fed them in cradles. As Garcilaso de la Vega writes,

> Every morning when [a baby] was wrapped up it was washed in cold water, and often exposed to the night air and dew. When the mother wanted to pamper her child, she would take the water into her mouth and then wash it all over, except the head, and especially the crown, which was never washed. It was said this accustomed the babies to cold and hardship, and also that it strengthened their limbs.[34]

Toddlers similarly experienced little comforting from their parents. When the children outgrew their cradles, they were placed into deep pits that served as playpens. A few rags or toys were thrown in with the children to help them entertain themselves while their parents worked.

When a child reached nine years of age, they began working with their parents part time. Boys shepherded llama herds and chased animals out of the fields where crops were grown; girls helped their mothers, sewing, preparing meals, and taking care of younger siblings. Children of commoners did not attend school, but instead served work apprenticeships that prepared them for adult life. When they reached age twenty-three, they became part of the regular Inca workforce.

CRIME AND PUNISHMENT

In such a highly regimented society, criminal behavior was simply not tolerated. In fact, however, there was very little crime in the Inca Empire because there was no motivation to steal. Money was neither needed nor recognized since the state provided everything a person needed to live. Moreover, the ownership among commoners of personal possessions such as jewelry was prohibited except under special circumstances. And the punishment for seemingly minor crimes, Prescott writes, was sure, swift, and severe:

> The crimes of theft, adultery, and murder were all capital; though it was wisely provided that some exten-

INCA NAMING PARTIES

In Inca society, babies were not named until they were weaned. At that time, the parents threw a festive ceremony called rutuchicoy *("hair cutting"). The names typically chosen were of animals, objects, or places that possessed desirable qualities, such as* Hawk *or* Puma. *Pedro de Cieza de León describes the tradition in his chronicles.*

"One thing I noticed while I was in these kingdoms of Peru was that in most of the provinces they had the custom of naming the children when they were fifteen or twenty days old, names which they had used until they were ten or twelve years old, and then, or some earlier, they received other names. When this was to be done, on a certain day set for this purpose, most of the relatives and friends of the father assembled, and danced as was their custom, and drank, which is their favorite pastime; and when the celebration had come to an end, one of them, the oldest and most respected, cut the hair of the boy or girl who was to be named, and the nails which, with the hair, were carefully put away. The names they give them and which they use are names of towns and birds, or plants, or fish. . . . The caciques [chiefs] and headmen pick names to their taste, and the best they can find, even though [the name] Atahuallpa means something like 'chicken.'"

uating circumstances might be allowed to mitigate the punishment. . . . Blasphemy against the Sun, and malediction of the Inca—offences, indeed, of the same complexion—were also punished with death. . . . Rebellion against the "Child of the Sun" was the greatest of all crimes.[35]

After a crime was committed, a simple trial was held that allowed everyone involved to present his or her case. The civil administrator in the area acted as judge and dispensed justice according to the laws of the province if the offense was a minor one. Capital cases, however, had to be turned over to the provincial governor since he was the only one allowed to issue the death penalty. Punishment in such cases could include being stoned, thrown into a pit with poisonous snakes, or clubbed on the back of the head.

THE DOCTORS USED COMMON SENSE AND MAGIC

Clearly, an Inca's life was hard, and—unless an individual was lucky—it tended to be short. When someone fell ill, treatments were often combinations of common sense and magic. Treatments varied from one part of the empire to another, depending on local beliefs. Some Incas believed that illnesses had supernatural causes and could only be treated by priests who performed different rituals and sacrifices. Others used plants and herbs to treat illnesses but resorted to superstition if nothing else worked.

HERBAL REMEDIES AND SURGERY

Sometimes herbal remedies were ineffective and other treatments were needed. Bloodletting was one of the most common cures. A sharp piece of stone was used to pierce an artery close to where a person said the pain was felt. The blood was allowed to flow from the artery until the supposed poisons were bled out. Purging was used to relieve sluggishness. Herbalists created a mixture from ground roots that was used to purge the impurities thought to be responsible for the illness. Garcilaso de la Vega wrote from firsthand experience that the cure could be just as bad as the illness:

> They feel as if ants were swarming over their arms and legs, in their veins and sinews and over all the body. Evacuation is almost always by both ways. While it lasts, the patient is giddy and sick, and anyone who

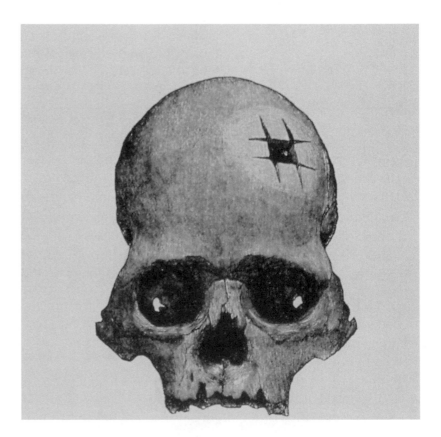

This Inca skull shows evidence of trepanning, a technique that released pressure from a patient's head through a hole in the skull.

had not experienced the effects of the root would think that they were dying. The patient has no wish to eat or drink. He expels all his humors, and readily yields up worms and other vermin that breed inside.[36]

Inca healers occasionally attempted surgery when all other treatments failed. Some tribes within the Inca realm practiced trepanning, which was a surgical technique used to treat severe head injuries. Trepanning involved cutting a hole in the skull to relieve pressure on the brain caused by a blow to the head, usually from a weapon like a mace or cudgel. Trepanning probably killed many patients, but experts have found trepanned skulls that show edges that had healed over time, indicating that the patient survived the surgery.

Chapter

5 The Last of the Great Kings

Topa Inca Yupanqui died after a long and prosperous reign. His son Huayna Capac, whose name meant "Young King with Many Virtues," was chosen out of sixty-two sons by the *orejones* of Cuzco to succeed his father.

Huayna became the eleventh ruler of the Inca Empire and one of the last kings to expand its vast boundaries. Huayna was described by Spanish chronicler Pedro de Cieza de León as "not large of stature, but strong and well built, of grave, goodly countenance, a man of few words and many deeds."[37] Huayna was also young and sometimes imprudent in his actions, so he was advised by his mother, whose words were said to influence many of his decisions. With her help, Huayna Capac continued the work of his father and grandfather.

Under Huayna Capac, the growth of the empire proved to be much slower since the Incas had already conquered most of the other tribes in the region. Just controlling the provinces that had already been conquered occupied much of Huayna's time. But under the Incas' inheritance laws, Huayna needed to add to his own holdings since most of the good land was still owned by his dead father

and grandfather. The empire was bordered by the ocean to the west, inhospitable deserts to the south, and swamps and forestlands occupied by fierce tribes to the east. Huayna decided to leave the

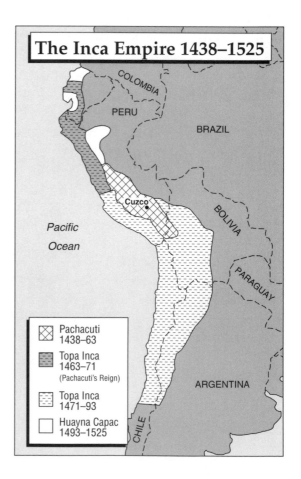

The Inca Empire 1438–1525

COLOMBIA

PERU

BRAZIL

Cuzco

BOLIVIA

Pacific Ocean

PARAGUAY

ARGENTINA

CHILE

⊠ Pachacuti 1438–63

▦ Topa Inca 1463–71 (Pachacuti's Reign)

⬚ Topa Inca 1471–93

☐ Huayna Capac 1493–1525

Amazon tribes to the south and east alone and focused his attention north. He summoned the Inca army and headed north toward what today is Ecuador, leading a column of men said to number two hundred thousand.

THE SECOND INCA CAPITAL

Huayna Capac had always been drawn to the lush forests of Ecuador; in fact, he had been born in the region during one of his father's northern campaigns. Huayna built a fabulous palace in Tumibamba, which is now the Ecuadorian city of Cuenca. He took a Quito princess as a bride and sired a son, who would become the last ruler of the empire. Huayna built up Tumibamba until it was second only to Cuzco in royal splendor.

Huayna had always been known for his love of women and drinking. He stayed at his northern refuge for years since it allowed him to enjoy a lifestyle that would have been frowned on in Cuzco. In Tumibamba, Huayna was not accountable to the *orejones,* who after all had placed him on the throne.

Huayna advanced his armies all the way to the Ancasmayo River but stopped after he encountered savage resistance by Pasto Indians in what today is Colombia. The Incas were able to eventually defeat the Pasto, but then an uprising in Ecuador by the recently conquered Cayambi people forced Huayna to halt his drive north. He had golden stakes driven into the earth to mark the edge of the empire on what today is the border between Ecuador and Colombia.

THE FORESTS ARE SLICK WITH INCA BLOOD

The Cayambi were cannibals who objected to the laws that forbade them from indulging in their traditional practices. They secretly plotted with other tribes in the region to overthrow Inca control. Garcilaso de la Vega writes that the rebels planned to attack an Inca garrison and slay the provincial governor:

> The day arrived, and the natives butchered them with the greatest cruelty, offering their heads, hearts and blood to their own gods in gratitude for having freed them from the Inca's sway and restored their ancient customs. They ate the flesh of all their victims with great voracity and relish, swallowing it unchewed as a result of having been forbidden to touch it for so long under the pain of punishment if they did so.[38]

Huayna Capac was so angered by the attack that he ordered his army to avenge the slain Incas "with blood and fire."[39] The Cayambi were driven back to their strongholds by the fury of the attack. Then, using an old Inca trick, Huayna and part of the army feigned retreat to draw the Cayambi out of their fortresses in pursuit. The second half of the Inca army then closed in, cutting off the Cayambi's retreat. The Cayambi continued to fight, despite being surrounded, and took the lives of many Incas. After the Cayambi were defeated, Huayna had all of the prisoners beheaded and thrown into a lake, which is now known as Yahuarcocha ("the Lake

THE LOST CITY

On July 24, 1911, a young American named Hiram Bingham discovered a lost Inca city that had been left untouched (even by the Spanish) for five centuries. It was called Machu Picchu, which is Quechua for "Old Mountain," and it sat on a granite mountaintop fifty miles northwest of Cuzco. John Hemming describes Bingham's discovery in his book Machu Picchu.

"There, amid the dark trees and tangled undergrowth, he saw building after building, including a three-sided temple whose granite blocks were cut with amazing beauty and precision. 'I suddenly found myself in a maze of beautiful granite houses!' Bingham would later write of this ecstatic moment. And, as he investigated each successive archaeological treasure in this lost city set on its steep, forested ridge, he observed, 'They were covered with trees and mosses and the growth of the centuries, but in the dense shadow, hiding in bamboo thickets and tangled vines, could be seen, here and there, walls of white granite ashlars most carefully cut and exquisitely fitted together.' Bingham's expedition was only a few days old and already it had unearthed what are certainly the most famous ruins in all of South America, Machu Picchu."

The most famous ruins in all of South America, Machu Picchu.

of Blood"). Despite the harshness with which the Cayambi rebellion was punished, this would not be the last challenge to Huayna's rule.

Another uprising involved the treachery of a chieftain from the island of Puná in the Gulf of Guayaquil. The chieftain conspired with his allies to kill Huayna Capac and his generals. Gifts were sent to the *sapa* Inca with an invitation to visit Puná. Rafts were provided to the island, but several trips had to be made to accommodate the large number of Inca visitors. Once the islanders were beyond sight of the shore, they cut the lashings that held the raft together and dropped the Inca nobles into the water. The islanders killed the floundering men with weapons they had hidden on themselves. After the last Inca was killed, the islanders reassembled the rafts. They returned to the shore to pick up the next group, which was unaware of the deadly fate of its peers. Huayna was angered by the slaughter of his kinsmen and ordered immediate reprisals. Thousands of islanders, including those suspected of participating in the conspiracy, were tortured and killed.

The eleventh ruler of the Inca Empire, Inca Huayna Capac (pictured), was chosen out of more than sixty-two sons to succeed his father, Topa Inca Yupanqui.

THE BEARDED ONES

While recovering from his campaigns, Huayna Capac received news of strange men who had recently appeared in the coastal city of Tumbes. The frightened messenger reported that the strangers had pale skin and beards like the god Viracocha was said to have. They wore silver coats, he said, and carried thunder in their hands, walking freely through the town and pilfering any valuables they could find. Huayna refused to believe what he was hearing and made the messenger retell the story several times. Another *chasqui* arrived shortly afterward and reported that the strangers had departed in a wooden house on the sea and had left two men behind. Huayna sent the *chasqui* back to tell his provincial governor to bring the two bearded men back to him. In the meantime, Huayna retreated to his chambers, recalling a prophecy he had heard that involved strangers who would destroy both the empire and the religion of its inhabitants.

AN INVISIBLE ENEMY STALKS THE LAND

The two bearded men were never found, which greatly concerned Huayna. He could not help wondering if the prophecies were coming true. A string of ill omens beset the empire: Three rings were seen encircling the moon, and a green comet crossed the heavens. The most startling omen occurred during the celebration of the Incas' most important festival,

Inti Raymi ("Festival of the Sun"). Garcilaso de la Vega later wrote of this event:

> They saw a royal eagle, which they call anca, approach, pursued by five or six kestrels and other little hawks. . . . These in turn fell on the eagle, brought it down and dealt it mortal blows. The eagle could not defend itself and sought refuge by dropping into the middle of the main square of the city, among the Incas. The latter picked it up and found it stricken and covered with scales, like a scurf [a scaly desposit], and almost denuded of its under feathers. They fed it and tried to cure it, but to no avail, and within a few days it died, unable to rise from the ground.[40]

The emperor had his royal guard doubled and ordered sacrifices performed. Likewise, the priests and soothsayers were asked to consult their oracles to divine the meaning of this new omen.

MANY STRANGE DEATHS ARE REPORTED

Huayna was shaken by the eagle incident, which seemed to coincide with the reports of many mysterious deaths throughout the empire. An Inca legend relates the visit of a dark messenger to Huayna one night. The messenger, whose face was hidden beneath a cloak, handed the ruler a box and left without saying a word. Huayna opened the box, releasing a swarm of moths. The moths flew around the room and disappeared out the windows. Illness was said to have spread shortly afterward.

Experts believe that the illness that swept the empire was smallpox and/or measles, which were diseases brought to the New World by Europeans, and against which the people of the Americas had no resistance. The disease spread south from Panama into Colombia and Ecuador, killing thousands. Huayna would never know that he and his army had fulfilled the prophecy of the cloaked messenger by bringing the diseases with them to Cuzco, thereby killing thousands, including his *coya* and others in the royal family. Hundreds of thousands of commoners, nobles, and royals alike died throughout the empire. Even the son of the sun was not immune to the disease, as Huayna fell ill. Sacrifices were made by the high priest but not even the *capaccocha* could help Huayna Capac.

In his study of Inca history, Garcilaso writes that before Huayna died, he summoned the royal family, his generals, and the *orejones* to his palace and told them of the dire predictions that had been made about the end of the empire:

> Many years ago it was revealed to us by our father the Sun that after twelve of his sons had reigned, a new race would come, unknown in these parts, and would gain and subdue all our kingdoms and many others to their empire. . . . They will be a brave people who will overcome us in everything. We also know that in my reign the number of twelve Incas is completed. I assure you that a few years

The Arrival of the Viracochas

The pale complexion of the Europeans came as quite a shock to the Incas, who all had dark hair and dark complexions. Because the Indians' gods were described as bearded and pale, the Incas thought they were coming face to face with their makers and let their guards down. In his Letter to a King, *Huamán Poma writes of the culture shock both the Spanish and the Indians experienced.*

"Atahuallpa and his nobles were amazed at what they heard of the Spaniards' way of life. Instead of sleeping, these strangers mounted guard at night. They and their horses were supposed to nourish themselves on gold and silver. They apparently wore silver on their feet, and their arms and their horses' bits and shoes were also reputed to be silver. . . . To our Indian eyes, the Spaniards looked as if they were shrouded like corpses. Their faces were covered with wool, leaving only the eyes visible, and the caps which they wore resembled little red pots on top of their heads. Sometimes they also decorated their heads with plumes. Their swords appeared very long, since they had to be carried with the points turned in a backward direction. They were all dressed alike and talked together like brothers and ate at the same table. Only one of them seemed to have powers of command and he had a dark face, white teeth and flashing eyes."

after I have gone away from you, these new people will come and fulfill what our father the Sun has foretold, and will gain our empire and become masters of it. I bid you obey them and serve them as men who will be completely victorious, for their law will be better than ours and their arms more powerful and invincible than ours.[41]

Ninan Cuyuchi was the rightful heir to the throne. Ninan had proven his worthiness to be emperor by standing by his father during the difficult campaigns in Ecuador. But Ninan fell ill and died before his father did. Huayna was made to chose between his sons Huáscar, the next in line, and his beloved son Atahuallpa. Before he died, Huayna divided the empire and gave Huáscar the southern half with its capital at Cuzco, while Atahuallpa received the northern half with its capital in Quito.

The Empire Is Divided

After Huayna's death, he was mourned for ten days. Then his heart was removed and placed in the temple in Quito while his mummified body was returned to Cuzco. The remains were placed in the Temple of the Sun with those of the other Inca rulers. Four thousand of Huayna's loyal retainers killed themselves so that they could accompany their king into the afterlife. Many more women were said to have hanged themselves in grief.

Despite Huáscar's repeated summons, Atahuallpa remained in Quito with his father's favored generals and much of the Inca army. Atahuallpa instead sent messengers to Cuzco with gifts. Huáscar killed four of the messengers and then cut off the noses of the remaining four, tearing their clothing down to their waists and sending them back to Atahuallpa. Huáscar then sought and imprisoned members of his father's royal court. He wondered if the reason his brother had not returned to Cuzco to pay him homage was because Atahuallpa was plotting to overthrow his rule. Huáscar tortured his prisoners to determine whether this was true. He even had members of his harem killed because he suspected that they were involved in a conspiracy. The visiting dignitaries and *curacas* that had come to pay their respects to the emperor fled from Huáscar's rage.

Huáscar sent emissaries to Quito to induce his half brother to return to Cuzco, but Atahuallpa knew that if he appeared in Cuzco he would be killed. At least in Quito, he possessed power and an army that would stand with him. After consulting with his generals, Atahuallpa declared himself king of Quito, an empire now separate from Cuzco.

Upon his death, Capac divided the Inca Empire in two, giving his son Huáscar (pictured) the southern half with its capital at Cuzco.

A WAR BETWEEN BROTHERS

The two brothers ruled their separate kingdoms for several years. Then Huáscar, who could not stand having half of his kingdom ruled by what he considered his rogue brother, sent one of his trusted generals, Atoc, and two thousand men to Quito. Huáscar was confident that members of the Cañari tribe, who had loyally served Cuzco's rulers for many years, would also join his forces. In response to the attack, Atahuallpa sent his generals, Quizquiz and Chaloguchima. The two

THE ORIGIN OF THE NAME *PERU*

According to Mestizo chronicler Garcilaso de la Vega, the name Peru *was neither a Spanish word nor a Quechuan one. In his* Royal Commentaries of the Incas, *Garcilaso explains that the name resulted from the confused answers of a captured Indian and the distortion of his words by his Spanish captors.*

"Having petted him to help him overcome his fear at the sight of their beards and unaccustomed clothes, the Spaniards asked him by signs and words what it was and what it was called. The Indian understood that they were asking him something from the gestures and grimaces they were making with hands and face, as if they were addressing a dumb man, but he did not understand what they were asking, so he told them what he thought they wanted to know. Thus fearing they might do him harm, he quickly replied by giving his own name, saying, 'Berú,' and adding another, 'pelú.' He meant: 'If you're asking my name, I'm called Berú, and if you're asking where I was, I was in the river.' The Christians understood what they wanted to understand, supposing the Indian had understood them and had replied as pat [firmly] as if they had been conversing in Spanish; and from that time, which was 1515 or 1516, they called that rich empire Peru, corrupting both words."

generals and the army they commanded were veterans of many wars during the reign of Huayna Capac. Atoc, on the other hand, had a poor military record and led an army of inexperienced conscripts. The two armies engaged in a bloody battle. Atoc's army was joined by the Cañari, as Huáscar had predicted, but even with their help, Atoc could not defeat the armies of Quizquiz and Chaloguchima. Atoc was captured and Atahuallpa had his skull turned into a goblet for *chicha* and his skin flayed and turned into a drum. Although this was the traditional fate of the defeated foes of the Incas, this was the first time the custom had been applied to another Inca.

Many battles followed between the two brothers, but the experienced northern army was able to defeat every army that Huáscar could summon. The armies of Atahuallpa were growing and marching closer to Cuzco with every victory. Huáscar appealed to the subject kingdoms of the Colla, Canchi, Chanca, and Condesuyu for men to meet this scourge that was trying to take the kingdom from its rightful heir.

ATAHUALLPA IS VICTORIOUS

The armies of Atahuallpa and Huáscar met and clashed in Chinchaysuyos. Thousands died on the first day, but neither side was able to gain advantage over the other. On the second day, Huáscar's general Huanca Auqui overran the northerners' positions, forcing the northern generals to order a retreat. Huáscar's army quickly encircled them and set fire to the dry grass. Many of Atahuallpa's soldiers were burned alive, though Quizquiz and his lieutenant managed to escape with a few thousand men. Huanca Auqui wanted to pursue the renegade army, but an overconfident Huáscar instead ordered his men to rest and savor the inevitable victory that would end Atahuallpa's reign.

Quizquiz and Chaloguchima took advantage of this respite by regrouping their forces. They sent spies into the enemy camp and discovered that Huáscar would be joining his men to witness the final blow. The two generals formulated a plan to capture Huáscar. The following day, Huanca Auqui led an advance patrol into a gorge where Atahuallpa's men were thought to be. As soon as the general appeared, Quizquiz and his men silently ambushed and killed Huanca Auqui's guards. The general was quickly taken away to serve as a hostage.

Huáscar and his entourage arrived shortly afterward. When Huáscar saw the bodies of the slain men, he immediately ordered a retreat, but it was too late. General Chaloguchima emerged with half of the army and attacked. Quizquiz came up from behind with the other half of the army and blocked their retreat. Huáscar's guards and litter bearers were killed, and Huáscar was pulled off of his golden litter onto the ground. General Chaloguchima took Huáscar's place on the litter and rode back to Huáscar's camp. When Huáscar's army saw that Chaloguchima had taken Huáscar's litter, they dropped their weapons and fled in terror.

A NEW EMPEROR IS CROWNED

Quizquiz and Chaloguchima stopped outside of Cuzco. A *chasqui* was sent into the capital to tell the *orejones* that the dispute between the two brothers and their armies was over. Everyone would be pardoned if they came out and swore fealty to Atahuallpa. The *orejones* discussed the matter amongst themselves for a day before coming out to meet the generals. For their participation in the war, some of Huáscar's generals were killed by a blow to the back of the head. The rest of the group had their arms and feet bound and were made to face the direction of the new emperor. They were taunted and forced to pluck their own eyebrows in offering. Huáscar's mother, Mama Rahua Occlo, publicly denounced her son.

Quizquiz sent a *chasqui* to tell Atahuallpa that the people of Cuzco had submitted to his rule. Huáscar was taken in chains to Cuzco to be paraded before his former subjects. His concubines were brought before him and were hanged in front of his eyes.

Atahuallpa left Quito and headed for Cuzco to claim the royal fringe. On his

Emperor Atahuallpa's supporters lead Huáscar into the capital in this seventeenth-century illustration.

with 168 men and Indian auxiliaries, who had been picked up along the way. Pizarro sent one of his lieutenants, Hernando de Soto, to scout ahead. De Soto returned a week later with an emissary from Atahuallpa who bore gifts and an invitation to meet in the city of Cajamarca. Pizarro accepted the invitation and sent the messenger back with gifts in return.

The Spaniards took a treacherous route through mountains to avoid being ambushed. They clawed up trails so steep they had to dismount from their horses. As historian Philip Ainsworth Means writes, "Every step of the way was full of danger which quite failed to daunt the Castilians and full also of occasions upon

Francisco Pizarro begins his perilous ascent up the Andes to meet Atahuallpa.

way to Cuzco, he stopped to consult with an oracle, who made a prophecy that foretold his death. Atahuallpa killed the priest in anger and left. But before reaching the capital, a messenger caught up to his procession and reported that the silver-plated bearded men had returned and that they now rode strange animals that resembled large sheep.

AN APPOINTMENT WITH THE EMPEROR

One of these bearded men was none other than the Spanish explorer Francisco Pizarro, who had arrived at the coastal city of Tumbes and was continuing south which Atahuallpa might have, but did not, hurl his warriors upon them to crush them. Instead of doing so, he sent them handsome gifts and generally beckoned them on."[42] They arrived at Cajamarca in a week and descended into the valley where thousands of colorful tents blanketed the mountainside. Chroniclers estimate that between thirty to eighty thousand warriors were camped around their emperor. Atahuallpa patiently awaited the strangers' arrival near the hot springs outside of town.

Pizarro sent de Soto and twenty men to ride out to the Inca camp to announce their arrival. The Spaniards tried to disguise their fear as they walked through the vast Inca encampment. De Soto noticed that Atahuallpa and his generals were looking at the Spaniards' horses with undisguised awe. In an attempt to intimidate the Inca ruler, de Soto charged Atahuallpa and reared his horse in front of the stony-faced Inca. Atahuallpa did not flinch.

De Soto was impressed by how disciplined and well equipped the Inca army was. Atahuallpa had agreed to meet with Pizarro the following day, which gave the Spaniards time to prepare. Atahuallpa had ordered Cajamarca abandoned before they arrived so that they had free run of the town. As night fell, the Spaniards could see the many fires of the Inca camp. Pizarro tried to lift the faltering spirits of his men with reassurances: "The Governor exhorted them to make fortresses of their hearts since they had no other, and no other help except from God who aids his servants in their greatest need."[43]

6 A Historic Encounter

Francisco Pizarro and his men got very little sleep, but they did not feel their exhaustion. Their hands shook in anticipation and fear of what was to come. Pizarro had formulated a daring plan the night before to capture the Inca ruler. He ordered his men to conceal themselves in the empty buildings and stay mounted on their horses. He sent lookouts armed with large, heavy guns called harquebuses up to the Inca fortress that overlooked the town. They waited with their weapons at the ready and prayed for the strength and courage to succeed.

The emperor's servants appeared in the town square first, sweeping the road ahead of the royal caravan with brooms. Hundreds of singers, dancers, and musicians followed, singing songs of triumph that one soldier later said "sounded like the songs from hell!"[44] When Atahuallpa finally appeared, he was being held high over the heads of his bearers on a golden litter. He regally sat on a throne made of gold that was trailed by brightly colored parrot feathers. Noblemen marched alongside wearing a dazzling array of gold and silver jewelry. Five or six thousand nobles and servants squeezed into the plaza. Atahuallpa looked around puzzled and asked where the strangers were.

Vicente de Valverde, a Dominican friar, emerged from his hiding place accompanied by an Indian interpreter named Felipe. He held a prayer book in one hand and a crucifix in the other. The friar told Atahuallpa that they were the ambassadors of a distant emperor, who served a *capac* (king) greater than the Inca himself. The Spanish *capac* required that Atahuallpa renounce his heathen beliefs and submit to him. Most of Valverde's speech was lost in the translation since Felipe's understanding of Spanish was very basic. However, Atahuallpa understood enough to know that the strangers were asking the son of the sun to relinquish his power and defer to a mere man. Atahuallpa responded by saying that these lands had been won by his father, Huayna Capac, who had handed them down to Huáscar. And since Huáscar had been defeated, they were now his.

Atahuallpa demanded to see the object that was being waved at him, and he snatched the Bible from Valverde's hands. Atahuallpa opened the book and saw what looked like pressed cocoa leaves. The friar urged the Inca ruler to let the book speak to him. Atahuallpa placed his ear against the pages to listen to this minor *huaca* speak, but he heard nothing. He threw the Bible down into the dirt with contempt. He had destroyed idols more powerful than this. Valverde scooped up the prayer book and retreated into the shadows, beckoning the conquistadores to attack.

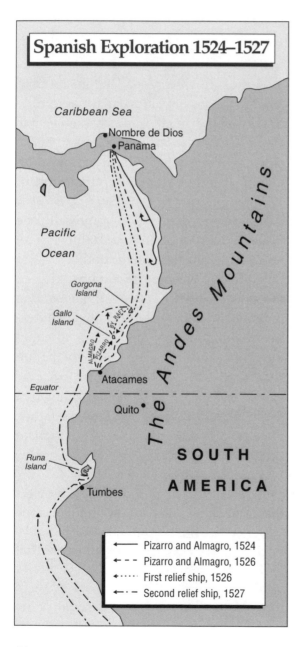

Spanish Exploration 1524–1527

Caribbean Sea

Nombre de Dios
Panama

Pacific Ocean

The Andes Mountains

Gorgona Island

Gallo Island

ALMAGRO
PIZARRO
BY RAFT

Atacames

Equator

Quito

Runa Island

SOUTH AMERICA

Tumbes

← Pizarro and Almagro, 1524
←- - Pizarro and Almagro, 1526
←···· First relief ship, 1526
←-·- Second relief ship, 1527

THE WAR FOR THE EMPIRE

Pizarro waved a white scarf, which signaled the attack. Explosions seemed to ring out from everywhere as guns and cannon were fired. Spanish war cries erupted from doorways, "Santiago! Santiago!" They were followed by a furious charge of mounted and running conquistadores brandishing lances and raised swords. The Inca ruler had been so confident of his superior numbers that his group had come unarmed. The terrified Incas tried to escape, but the plaza was too tightly packed. Horses trampled many of Atahuallpa's procession, and gunfire rained down on them from the towers. The exits were blocked by the bodies of the slain. The panicking Incas could do nothing but press against the walls lining the square to avoid being trampled. One wall collapsed under the weight being pressed against it and allowed the routed Incas to flee through the breach. The Spanish horsemen pursued them until they were recalled by trumpet.

The fighting intensified around Atahuallpa as the Spaniards tried to end the battle by killing him. The nobles rallied around their beloved leader and threw themselves in front of all harm. They were all unarmed and were thus cut down as quickly as they could step forward to support Atahuallpa's litter. The Inca ruler soon fell to the earth. The anxious conquistadores pressed forward. Pizarro was determined to capture Atahuallpa alive, and he parried a blow meant for Atahuallpa. The conquistadores quickly ushered Atahuallpa into a nearby building, where they held him as a hostage.

capture of Atahuallpa, the mighty empire was paralyzed. Without their leader to guide them, the Incas did what they had learned to do since birth: They waited for orders. In the meantime, Atahuallpa was placed under heavy guard and was treated well by his Spanish captors. He was even allowed visits from his subjects who had returned to Cajamarca and had restored their lives in town as if nothing had happened.

During Atahuallpa's imprisonment, he learned of the Spaniards' consuming lust for gold and silver. He made a deal with Pizarro, promising that his cell would be filled with stacks of gold and twice that of silver if the Spaniards would agree to

Spanish chronicler Poma de Ayala's drawing depicts Pizarro setting aflame the Incas' temporary refuge.

After ordering his brother's death, Emperor Atahuallpa reigned over the entire Inca Empire.

Before entering Cajamarca, Atahuallpa had ordered his top general, Rumiñaui, to block the passages out of the valley and to converge on the city if signaled. "But the roar of the artillery—the mountains vibrated to its echoes—and the furious gallop of the horses told Rumiñaui that the game was up and that the signal would never come."[45] Suspecting an inevitable defeat, Rumiñaui and his army retreated to Quito.

COLLECTING A RANSOM

The Inca Empire demanded unquestioning obedience from its subjects. Therefore, thinking for one's self was discouraged and even punished. As a result, after the release him. Pizarro enthusiastically agreed to the terms and sent his men to accompany Atahuallpa's envoys as they traveled around the empire assembling the ransom. The group traveled from shrine to shrine, sacrilegiously stripping the walls of their gold and silver. Because of the immense distances that had to be traveled and the amount of gold that had to be transported, the ransom trickled in over months in llama caravans from all over the empire. Prescott notes,

> On some days, articles of the value of thirty or forty thousand pesos de oro were brought in, and occasionally, of the value of fifty or even sixty thousand pesos. The greedy eyes of the Conquerors gloated on the shining heaps of treasure, which were transported on the shoulders of the Indian porters. . . . But, as their avarice was sharpened by the ravishing display of wealth, such as they had hardly dared to imagine, they became more craving and impatient.[46]

As the ransom was being collected, rumors circulated about a revolt by the Incas. The Spanish suspected that the Incas were slowing the ransom collection in order to regroup their armies and launch an attack. Atahuallpa was thought to be at the center of the plot, but the Inca ruler assured the Spaniards that he was sincere about the ransom; Atahuallpa even suggested that the conquistadores send more of their own men out to speed up the flow of gold to Cajamarca.

Pizarro's brother, Hernando, took some men on patrol to the neighboring village of Guamachuato, where an army was rumored to be massing. They found no troops or any evidence of a revolt. Hernando then proceeded to Pachacamac, which was the home of a very powerful oracle. Atahuallpa had mentioned that it was the most revered shrine in the region and therefore received much tribute. The trip through the mountains was so rough that it wore out the horseshoes of the Spaniards' mounts. Since there was no iron available, Hernando had the metalsmiths of the village make replacement horseshoes out of silver. When they reached the temple, Hernando and his men pushed past the temple guardians and burst into the shrine. Instead of finding a room full of gold, their nostrils were assailed by the rank smells of sacrifice. The great oracle was a small *huaca* that sat in an empty, blood-stained room. The priests refused to tell where they had hidden the gold, so Hernando destroyed the idol and built a cross to put in its place.

Another party of conquistadores was sent to Cuzco. The inhabitants of Cuzco had heard of the Spaniards' arrival and thought they were gods who had come to save them from Atahuallpa. But the conquistadores strode past the waiting welcome party and, to the Incas' dismay, plundered the Coricancha. They removed hundreds of plates of gold and silver and tried to pry loose ornaments that had been permanently set into the walls.

About this time, one of Francisco Pizarro's partners, Diego de Almagro, arrived from Panama with 150 additional men, just in time to claim his share of the fabulous ransom. A third partner, Fer-

THE CONQUISTADOR AND THE INCAS

The general rule of the Inca Empire was subordination to one's superior. Every person abided by this rule and was punished for disobedience. The system worked well for the Incas but created generations of followers who could not function on their own. When the Spanish arrived and killed their emperor, the Incas did not know how to react. In his book Peru, *Sir Robert Marett describes the differences between the Incas and the conquistador that led to this end.*

"It is scarcely possible to conceive of two peoples so utterly different in character as the Peruvian Indians and their Spanish conquerors. . . . What a contrast there is between the cautious approach to life of the Indians and the reckless gambler's spirit of the Spanish conquerors. To the Spaniards, endowed with a superabundance of initiative and daring, life was a lottery. The Inca established their empire step by step through a systematic combination of conquest and diplomacy. But there was nothing systematic about the Spanish conquest of the New World. The initiative came from a handful of remarkable individuals who as often as not acted in conflict with Spanish officialdom. An important motive of these adventurers was no doubt thirst for gold and booty. . . . But the conquistadors were far more than piratical merchant adventurers. Just as much as by greed they were motivated by a combination of missionary zeal—the desire to conquer and convert the infidel for the glory of God—and a love of adventure. . . . 'Conquest fired their imagination by its quixotic element.' They were 'in love with glory.'"

nando Luque, had died before Almagro left Panama, leaving Almagro and Pizarro to split their booty. Pizarro and his men did not believe that Almagro was entitled to half, however, since he had not participated in the capture of Atahuallpa. This disagreement opened a rift between the surviving partners.

Historian John Hemming writes that the huge amount of gold was turned into ingots, and for the first time in their lives, the Incas were subjected to slavery: "On May 3 Francisco Pizarro had ordered his men to begin the enormous task of melting down more than 11 tons of gold objects and 26,000 pounds of silver. Native laborers were forced to toil over the furnaces, breaking up and crushing objects fed into them. On a good day the workers were able to melt down 600 pounds of metal."[47] The most delicate golden art pieces were sent back to Spain with Francisco Pizarro and a fifth of the total amount of gold. Each soldier received forty-five pounds of gold and ninety pounds of silver. The cavalrymen received a double share and

Pizarro, the appointed governor of Peru, took many times the cavalrymen's share.

THE EXECUTION OF ATAHUALLPA

Atahuallpa knew his time was short. The Spaniards had not released him after receiving their ransom. Likewise, the Inca ruler had been told that shooting stars and a greenish-black comet had been repeatedly seen in the night skies. These were all the same ill omens that Atahuallpa's father, Huayna Capac, had witnessed before he had died. Chronicler Garcilaso de la Vega wrote that Atahuallpa affirmed his fate to his generals:

> I am full of grief to realize that I am to die so soon, without having enjoyed the possession of my realms, for these signs only show themselves to announce some great calamity, the death of kings or destruction of empires. I suspected all this before when I found myself in iron chains, but the appearance of this comet has now assured me of it.[48]

When Pizarro learned that Atahuallpa had ordered his own brother's execution, he used this as an excuse to put the Inca sovereign on trial. Atahuallpa was quickly pronounced guilty of treason and murder and was sentenced to be burned at the stake. Friar Valverde, who was chosen to perform the last rites, offered Atahuallpa a last chance to accept Christianity. If Atahuallpa allowed himself to be baptized, the friar promised, he would receive a more merciful execution. Atahuallpa did

Pizarro orders Atahuallpa's execution. Prior to his death, Atahuallpa accepted Christianity and took the name Juan de Atahuallpa, in honor of John the Baptist.

not want to be deprived of mummification and the afterlife that would allow. He agreed to take the Christian name Juan de Atahuallpa in honor of John the Baptist, and he was then strangled with a cord in the central plaza of Cajamarca.

THE UNRAVELING OF THE EMPIRE

After Atahuallpa's death, the empire began to fall apart. Provinces that had chaffed under Inca rule took advantage of the situation and withdrew from the Inca Empire. The distribution system for food and clothing broke down; storehouses were looted, and their supplies were hoarded by the villagers. Pizarro quickly tried to restore order by selecting a puppet ruler who would give the appearance that Inca leadership and power still existed. Huáscar's brother Topa Huallpa was designated as emperor but was poisoned shortly after accepting the royal fringe.

Pizarro left Cajamarca on August 11, 1533, accompanied by almost five hundred men. Their destination was Cuzco, but the journey was another difficult trip through the mountains. Along the way the Spaniards kept alert for ambushes, but they encountered very little resistance, which surprised them. According to author Alfred Métraux,

> A strange apathy seems to have overcome the Indians. The army made no counterattack, nor did the Indians rise in mass to rescue the emperor and drive out the intruders. The aggressive inclinations of a few Inca chiefs was easily nipped in the bud or overcome. The Indians accepted the extractions and brutality of the Spanish soldiers with resignation and without apparent anger.[49]

When Pizarro and his men arrived in Cuzco, news of Atahuallpa's death had already reached the city. The Spaniards were greeted as liberators. Thousands of Cuzco's residents crowded the streets to watch their procession through the city. Garcilaso de la Vega writes that the Spaniards rode through Cuzco on litters borne by the Incas:

> They thus entered the city with great rejoicings; and its inhabitants came out with many songs and dances composed in praise of the Viracochas, for they were delighted to see their Inca, supposing that the legitimate heir was to rule and that Atahuallpa's cruelties were at an end. The streets along which the Inca passed was strewn with reeds, and triumphal arches were raised at intervals covered with flowers, as the Indians were in the habit of doing for their royal triumphs.[50]

The Spaniards were impressed by the Inca capital, though it fell short of the kingdom of gold they had expected to find. Despite their disappointment, the Spanish considered the buildings in the inner city to be equal if not superior to any that the conquistadores had seen at home in Spain.

THE NEW LORDS OF CUZCO

Pizarro and his officers took up residence in the royal palaces that had belonged to the past emperors, and the rest of his men camped in the central plaza. Pizarro ordered his men not to bother the people of the city, but greed overcame their fear of reprimand. They plundered the other royal palaces and tortured the nobles, trying to draw information about treasure they suspected had been hidden.

In the midst of the chaos, a young prince named Manco Inca Yupanqui, who was the half brother of Huáscar, approached Pizarro with an offer to collaborate with the Spanish. All he asked in return was to be given his rightful inheritance to be emperor. Pizarro agreed and arranged for Manco to be given the royal fringe in a lavish coronation that recalled the glory of times past.

THERE ARE MANY FORTUNES TO BE FOUND

News of Pizarro's success in Peru spread to Spain as well as to other Spanish colonies in the New World. Thousands of would-be adventurers, inspired by Pizarro's conquest, tried to make their way to the New World to make their own fortunes. The Holy Roman Emperor King Charles V tried to stop the flood of disreputable treasure hunters by allowing only colonists to travel to Peru.

Ignoring the king's wishes, the governor of Guatemala, Pedro de Alvarado, funded his own trip to Peru. He had been reading the reports of Pizarro's expeditions for years and knew that Pizarro had not yet conquered the northern half of the Inca Empire. Alvarado and his fleet landed in Ecuador, close to where Pizarro had landed on his way to Cajamarca. Alvarado commanded five hundred men along with four thousand Guatemalan Indian auxiliaries. They captured local Indians to use as guides and forced them to take the most direct route to Quito, which also happened to be the most treacherous. The local Indians escaped from Alvarado before reaching the frigid mountain passes. A quarter of Alvarado's men

and half of his Indian auxiliaries died as a result.

Alvarado and his men emerged from the mountains in poor shape. Adding to their disappointment, they discovered that Quito had already been visited by one of Pizarro's officers, Sebastián de Belalcázar. Belalcázar had heard of Alvarado's landing in Ecuador and rushed north with 140 men. Belalcázar beat Alvarado to Quito but found no gold. Instead, Belalcázar found and defeated Atahuallpa's general, Rumiñaui, who had deserted his emperor in Cajamarca. Alvarado eventually met with Belalcázar and agreed to sell him his fleet of ships and his supplies, and transfer command of his men to Pizarro in return for one hundred thousand pesos. Alvarado then returned to Guatemala.

Meanwhile, Hernando Pizarro went to Spain to present the royal court with another share of gold. He returned with more ships and men as well as new titles and a new division of lands for the two partners, including a governorship for Almagro. Francisco Pizarro was named marquis d'Altabillos and was granted the northern part of the Inca Empire, now called New Castile. Hernando Pizarro was made a knight of Santiago, and Almagro was granted control of the southern part of the empire, now called New Toledo. Even Friar Valverde was granted a new title for his contribution to the expedition: bishop of Cuzco. But the royal grants were vague and did not specify where Almagro's and Pizarro's territories ended, so the two temporarily agreed to share control of Cuzco.

Pizarro and Almagro then parted ways. Pizarro left Cuzco so he could build a new capital on the coast. Cuzco was too far inland to be useful for commerce and was too heavily populated with Indians. Pizarro established a new city six miles from the ocean, which he called Ciudad de los Reyes ("City of the Kings"), although in later years it would be known as Lima. Indian workers were brought from hundreds of miles away to work on the new city. Almagro, in turn, took 570 Spaniards and 12,000 Indians and set out to explore lands to the south.

The Indians Are Rebelling

Manco Inca Yupanqui served as a puppet ruler for two years and cooperated with the Spaniards by helping crush the revolts of Atahuallpa's followers. He stood idle while the Spaniards desecrated all of the sacred Inca shrines and violated the chosen women of the temples. Nobles were robbed in their own homes, and Incas were being enslaved in Cuzco as well as in the rest of the empire. Finally Manco determined that the time had come to reclaim the capital and restore the empire. He conspired with the Incas' high priest and with his generals to throw off Spanish rule. Messengers were sent to provinces all over the empire to mobilize troops.

Manco had been caught trying to slip out of the city by Indian collaborators in Cuzco who were hostile to the Incas. He was thrown in prison but managed to escape by bribing Hernando Pizarro. When Pizarro discovered what was afoot, he tried to recapture Manco. A patrol that had been sent to bring Manco back, however, returned unsuccessful. They reported that a large number of Incas was massing in the valley.

Hernando Pizarro and his brother Juan wasted no time in gathering their men, but the Spaniards were not only outnumbered, they were also divided. Many of the conquistadores in Cuzco were ill or wounded, and Almagro had taken a large number of troops on his expedition south. Francisco Pizarro was at his capital of Lima, but the Incas had cut communication between the cities so that the two Pizarro brothers had to defend Cuzco without help. Messengers continued to arrive, reporting that rebellion was flaring throughout the country.

Cuzco Under Siege

Hernando and Juan Pizarro only had two hundred conquistadores (less than half of whom had horses) and hundreds of Inca-hating Indian auxiliaries against two hundred thousand Inca warriors. The Spaniards knew that they could not survive a direct confrontation against such overwhelming numbers, so they barricaded themselves in the royal palaces. The Incas flooded into the narrow streets of the city and set traps. They had developed effective ways to combat the Spaniards' cavalry by digging spike-filled pits and small holes designed to catch a horse's hoof and break its legs.

Thinking that they could drive the Spaniards out of hiding, they hurled stones wrapped in burning cotton onto the thatched roofs of Cuzco, setting fire to the city. The smoke was so thick that the Spaniards almost died from asphyxiation. They retreated to the central plaza under a constant barrage of stones and were saved from burning to death when the fires inexplicably died.

The Spaniards broke out into the streets and attacked the Inca warriors with merciless cavalry charges. But the Spaniards slowly lost ground to the Incas, who ran across the tops of scorched, roofless walls out of the way of the horses. Garcilaso de

Spanish soldiers fall under a barrage of stones at the Inca fortress of Sacsahuaman. After sustaining heavy losses, the Spaniards eventually retook Sacsahuaman.

la Vega writes that the Spaniards would have been completely overrun if not for the efforts of the Indian auxiliaries, who braved stone missiles to help the conquistadores:

> On seeing this, many of the Spaniards themselves said that they were in such straits that they did not know what would have happened to them if it had not been for the help of those Indians who brought them maize, herbs and everything they needed to eat and to cure their wounds, and went without food themselves so their masters might eat, and served as spies and watchmen, warning the Spaniards day and night of their enemies' intentions by secret signs.[51]

The Indians continued to fling stones from behind the parapets of Sacsahuaman, which the Spaniards determined had to be retaken if Cuzco were to be held. The Spaniards charged up the hill to the fortress, using their shields to protect them from the barrage of stones and javelins. According to Hemming, "Manco's men kept up a heavy fire, but they could not stop this contingent from reaching the plateau above Cuzco, or, once there, from racing along the highway and then wheeling behind some hills to reach the parade ground at the foot of Sacsayhuaman's ramparts."[52] Juan Pizarro was killed by a stone while trying to break through the Inca defenses. The Spaniards finally reached the fortress and built scaling ladders. Many men died in the battle, but eventually they retook Sacsahuaman. They then proceeded to execute all of the captured Incas.

The rebellion lasted for a year, but Manco was not able to defeat the Spaniards. Experts believe that Manco's failure was due to his army of farmers, who did not have much combat experience, and the fact that many of the elite Inca officers had been killed during the civil war between Atahuallpa and Huáscar. Members of Manco's army also faced starvation and were forced to leave the battle to return to their fields. The remainder of Manco's army was dispersed by the return of Almagro from Chile. Manco himself escaped with a thousand followers and retreated into the Amazon wilderness of Vilcabamba.

THE SUPERIORITY OF THE TOLEDO BLADE

When they first encountered Pizarro and his tiny force, the Inca army had two hundred thousand men and an intimate knowledge of the land. Moreover, the army was supported by a complex network of supply depots and was led by experienced veterans of many wars. The question therefore arises as to how a small group of cavalrymen and foot soldiers defeated the largest and best-trained army on the continent. Experts say that Atahuallpa's overconfidence played a leading role. The Inca sovereign was so sure that his superior numbers would be enough to defeat the Spaniards that he did not anticipate being captured and held hostage against his own country. The result was the destruction of the Inca government from the top down. Atahuallpa's capture and execution also had a demoralizing effect on the population, which thought that its leader was divine and the empire invincible.

The Inca Empire had faced many enemies, but none of its experiences in battle had prepared it for combat against a technologically superior enemy like the Spanish. The Spanish had body armor that was proof against most Inca arms. Although the Spanish had harquebuses and cannon, neither was very practical in battle. Both weapons required a lot of work to load and prime, and they only offered a single shot before needing to be reloaded. One of the most effective weapons that the conquistadores had was the steel Toledo blade. Cotton armor was no match for the thrust of a Spanish sword.

7 Life Under Spanish Rule

Diego de Almagro and his men spent two years searching for riches in one of the driest deserts in the world. But the lands that had been granted to him by the Spanish Crown were found to be worthless. Angry and frustrated at his ill fortunes, Almagro returned to Cuzco, not to answer Francisco Pizarro's plea for help, but to claim the city as his own. Almagro also claimed that Lima fell within the territory granted to him by King Charles V.

The two partners faced off against each other on the battlefield before thousands of Indians who came to watch. Pizarro's army, which was larger and better equipped, easily defeated Almagro's soldiers and captured their leader. Almagro was taken back to Cuzco, where he stood trial and was sentenced to death.

Almagro's mestizo son vowed vengeance. In 1541 the last of the Almagro faction burst into the chambers of Pizarro and killed the sixty-three-year-old conqueror of Peru with a sword point to the throat. Author Jean Descola writes of how Pizarro's life ended:

> The assassins, once the blow was struck, were confounded. They had killed Pizarro! They made off like

Diego de Almagro prepares to fight Pizarro and claim Cuzco and Lima as his own.

thieves. No one dared to touch the corpse for fear of compromising himself. Finally a man from Trujillo and his wife dragged the corpse to the nearest church, wrapped it in a shroud, and buried it. But despite their anxious haste, they took time to envelope the Marquis in a great white mantle of the Order of Santiago and to fasten his spurs.[53]

THE LAST BASTION OF INCA RULE

Manco Inca Yupanqui and his nobles tried to recreate the Inca way of life—including all of its rituals—at their refuge in Vilcabamba. Manco had managed to save the golden image of the sun, which had been hidden from the Spaniards, and some of the mummies of his ancestors.

Manco knew that he could not defeat the Spaniards in a pitched battle, so he employed guerrilla tactics. His men used captured Spanish horses, armor, swords, and even guns to launch attacks against Spanish travelers and raids against cities along the Cuzco-Lima highway. He incited rebellion among the Indians and tortured collaborators. Manco became an inspiration to the Incas that had been enslaved by the Spanish, and he evaded capture until he was finally killed by members of the Almagro faction that had sought sanctuary with the small Inca state. Manco's ten-year-old son Sayri succeeded his father and was closely advised by the nobles because of his youth.

The Spaniards still considered Vilcabamba a threat to the safety of the Spanish colonies, but they had failed to bring down the hidden empire by force. Prince Philip of Spain encouraged a diplomatic negotiation. An Inca princess named Beatriz, who was also an aunt of Sayri, was enlisted as an intermediary to offer Sayri a pardon for any crimes he or his father had committed. She was also authorized to offer Sayri Francisco Pizarro's estates and a large annual stipend. In return, Sayri was to abandon Vilcabamba and live in Cuzco. The offering was small in comparison to what the Spanish would gain by Sayri's submission.

Sayri was warned by his advisers not to trust the Spaniards. As Garcilaso de la Vega writes,

> They consulted their omens by sacrificing animals, by watching the birds of the air by day and night, and by contemplating the sky. They looked to see if the sun was serene and bright or sad and darkened with cloud and mist which gave them a good or evil omen. They did not consult the Devil, for, as we have seen, he lost the power of speech in all the empire as soon as the sacraments of our Holy Mother Church of Rome entered in. Although the men were favorable, the captains had opposing views.[54]

Sayri disregarded his advisers' warnings and accepted the offer. He left for Lima on a litter and was welcomed to the city by thousands of Indians, who had come out to watch the last Inca emperor who would be borne above his subjects' heads. Sayri was wed to an Inca princess, Cusi Huarcay, who, like Sayri, was the grandchild of the Inca ruler Huáscar. The church normally frowned on the marriage of close relatives, but the viceroy and the king of Spain had received a special dispensation from Pope Julius III. Sayri was baptized and his name was changed to a long amalgamation of his father's name and the name of the viceroy's father: Don Diego Hurtado de Mendoza Inca Manco Capac Yupanqui.

VILCABAMBA FALLS

To the Spaniards' dismay, the guerrilla activity based in Vilcabamba did not disappear with the retirement of Sayri's rule. Titu Cusi, Sayri's half brother, claimed the fringe and resumed raiding local towns and attacking travelers just as his father had done. But he did not share his father's hatred of the Spaniards, and toward the end of his rule he signed a treaty that allowed both sides to peacefully coexist. He even allowed Catholic missionaries to enter Vilcabamba.

Tupac Amarú became ruler after his brother Titu died. Tupac wanted the Incas of Vilcabamba to return to a more traditional lifestyle, and he sought to sever all ties with the Spanish. Tupac opposed Christianity and had all churches and Christian symbolism destroyed. The new viceroy, Francisco de Toledo, had been ordered to settle conflicts as peacefully as possible and to resort to violence only when necessary. Toledo considered the recent attacks on the Spanish by Tupac to be a violation of the treaty and an excuse to destroy Vilcabamba once and for all. The viceroy sent an invasion force of 250 soldiers and 2,000 Indian auxiliaries, which captured the guerrillas' stronghold.

EXECUTION OF THE LAST *SAPA* INCA

The commander of the Spanish army sent men into the jungle to pursue the routed Inca commanders. They returned with the mummies of Manco Inca Yupanqui and Titu Cusi, which were then destroyed, and the golden image of the sun. Manarí Indians helped another patrol track Tupac Amarú deep into the Amazon. After winding down the Amazon River in rafts and fighting off hostile natives, the persistent Spaniards caught up to Tupac and his pregnant wife, who both seemed relieved to have been found. Tupac admitted that he preferred capture to spending more time in the forests.

Tupac was brought to Cuzco to face trial. Toledo hurried the judicial process with the intent to execute the Inca ruler. Tupac was sentenced to death and was taken to the central plaza riding a mule. A large guard of Cañari Indians accompanied him in case a rescue attempt was made by the Incas. Thirty thousand Indians crowded the streets and hills overlooking the city to watch the procession, crying and shouting at the injustice. Garcilaso de la Vega was present during the event and writes, "The Inca raised his right arm with his hand open, then brought it to his ear, and dropped it gradually to his right thigh. From this the Indians understood that they were being told to be silent, and the shouting and crying ceased."[55] Before his execution, Tupac was offered a chance to convert to Christianity. He accepted and was baptized with the name Pedro. He was then beheaded—in the same square where Atahuallpa had been strangled thirty-nine years earlier—and his head was put onto a pike in the central plaza, where it was secretly worshiped by the Indians at night.

The shadow empire of Vilcabamba had become the last vestige of Inca independence. It had given the defeated Indians hope that the old empire and traditions could be restored one day. Its downfall would become a harsh reminder of the life that would await them.

LIFE AFTER THE CONQUEST

Viceroy Toledo embarked on a campaign to banish Inca traditions and alter their history so it would appear that the Spanish had freed the native peoples from Inca tyranny. He traveled throughout the land destroying shrines, idols, and *quipus* wherever he found them. "In short, the Viceroy himself and certain associates . . . made it their business to anathematize the Inca dynasty in such a way that their fair name would perish and that it would become clear to every one that the King of Castile is 'legitimate Lord of these realms'."[56]

Toledo was not shy about adapting some of the Inca administrative machinery to his use. He reinstituted the Inca provincial system that had monitored and collected tribute from local villages, modifying it to work with the colonial government. Unlike the Incas, however, who took time to calculate a fair tax rate for each province, Toledo arbitrarily determined what each province would pay the colonial government.

Although Spain questioned the harsh treatment of the natives in Toledo's system, Philip Ainsworth Means notes that the Crown's concern for the welfare of the natives was flexible, especially when it would reduce Spain's cut of the profits. "It concerned itself more with saving the souls of people by 'Christianizing' them than it did with making their sojourn on this planet reasonably comfortable and happy."[57] In fact, to increase the flow of revenue to the royal coffers, Spain made it easier for colonists to open mines in the colony now known as Peru. Prospectors and adventurers from all over the world traveled to Peru in search of riches.

THE INCAS ARE INTRODUCED TO SLAVERY

Indians were forced to labor in these mines and on farms that had once been theirs under a system known as *encomienda*. The *encomienda*, or royal land grant system, was introduced to Peru by Francisco Pizarro. It was originally meant to entice conquistadores to stay in the country, rather than leave on the first ship bound for Spain. The *encomienda* system divided the land and rewarded conquistadores with control over a region that had native populations to draw from for labor; thus, conquistadores had a stake in the country and a reason to stay. One of the stipulations was that the *encomenderos*, as they were known, would have to live in the Spanish-held cities, to provide mutual

HISTORICAL METHODS

Much of what is known of the ancient Incas comes from archaeological evidence. Pottery shards, jewelry, tools, and fossil evidence allow archaeologists to reconstruct the lives of these early people. Researcher Thomas Ewbanks, quoted in People of the Andes, *by* James B. Richardson III, *points out the importance of studying these artifacts.*

"Whatever is to be known has to be drawn out of the ground; out of what the plough turns up; what mounds, graves and earth-works may disclose; and what architectural ruins may afford. These are the only archives remaining of the deeds and destinies of the old inhabitants of the hemisphere; and hence everything registered in them, however trifling under other circumstances it might be considered, has a value proportioned to the insight it may give into national or social habits and conditions."

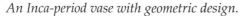
An Inca-period vase with geometric design.

protection, rather than living on their granted lands.

Another duty of the *encomenderos* was to provide the Indians under their control with Christian teachings. Some *encomenderos* took missionary work seriously and hired *doctrineros* (priests), of which the less reputable ones charged the Indians a fee on top of what the *encomenderos* were already paying them. They were known to rule their parishes with an iron hand and punished Indians who worshiped their old gods by torturing or imprisoning them. Between the fees of the *doctrineros*, the tribute to the *encomenderos*, and the additional taxes levied by the *curacas*, the Indians were left with no money to buy food or clothing. As a result, many Indians died of malnutrition. Inca chieftain Huamán Poma made an impassioned plea to the king of Spain and insisted that the Spaniards had no intention of fulfilling their Christian obligations: "At present the owners take no account of whether their workers are Christian or not. There is no religious instruction, no confession and no rest on Sundays and holidays, and no solemn Mass is sung for the souls of the dead."[58]

The problem with the *encomienda* system was that the Spanish enslaved entire communities of families, not just adult males, and subjected them to inhumane working conditions. The entire populations of some towns died in the mines. Viceroy Toledo had tried to curb this abuse by limiting the number of Indians that could be drawn from a region, but the mine owners blatantly ignored the law.

One of the solutions offered by Spain to prevent such abuses was the appointment of crown officials known as *corregidores*. *Corregidores* were district administrators who were responsible for collecting tribute. The *corregidores*, however, often did not have any concern for the hardship that such collections visited on the Indians. The *corregidores* themselves were often corrupt and supplemented their salaries by forcing the Indians to buy European goods that the Indians could not afford.

Locked Inside a Dark Mountain

After the Spanish monarch made it easier to open a mine in Peru, the mining industry doubled and then tripled in size. But because the native population had been steadily decreasing due to the diseases introduced by Europeans, mine owners were having trouble finding workers. Toledo then reinstated the Incas' *mita* system, which had required public service from each able-bodied male in the empire.

There was, however, a cruel difference in the *mita* under Spanish rule. In the original Inca system, the communities received food, clothing, and other services in return for their work; meanwhile, under the Spanish system the workers and their families received nothing in return for their labors. Historian John Hemming notes,

> Much of the tribute extracted during Inca times was stored for the welfare of the people, especially during times of crisis. The Indians were supported by the state while working, and they knew exactly how many days' labour would be required of them each year. Under the Spaniards, there was nothing to show for all the natives' work, and the only benefit was relief from military service in inter-tribal or expansionist wars. The Peruvians had been torn from the shelter of the benevolent, almost socialistic, absolute monarchy into the cruel world of feudal Europe.[59]

For the Indians forced to work in the mines, a dreadful fate awaited. The silver mine at Potosí was literally a mountain of silver, and the Indians were locked inside. The tunnels were pitch black and poorly ventilated. The Indians worked by candlelight and were made to climb frayed rope ladders with one-hundred-pound loads of ore on their backs. They worked with few breaks for a week at a time and slept and ate underground; they were only allowed out of the mine on Sundays. Wives worked side by side with their husbands and children and often witnessed the death of their overworked family members.

If Potosí was considered bad, the mercury mines at Huancavelica were far worse. The Spanish used mercury to draw silver from ore, but thousands of Indians died excruciating deaths from mercury poisoning. The toxic conditions inside the mountains decimated the population of the surrounding region. Although the reports of mistreatment of the workers caused the Spanish monarchy to order that only Indians who volunteered to work in the mines could be used, that order was overlooked when the flow of revenue back to Spain was threatened by lack of willing workers.

THE WORKERS REVOLT

The oppression of the Indians by the Spaniards continued for many years. Finally, in 1780, a descendant of Inca royalty named José Gabriel Condorcanqui, taking the name Tupac Amarú, led an uprising of sixty thousand peasants all over the former Inca domain. The rebels managed to take control of southern Peru and Bolivia, but with no training as a military leader, Tupac was eventually captured. He was taken to Cuzco and was tortured and executed in the central plaza.

MAKING THE INDIANS EQUALS

Some concerned Spaniards took it upon themselves to improve the lot of the Indians by educating them so that they could function in what was now Spanish society. Friar Domingo de Santo Tomás, the leader of the movement, studied the Incas' native language, Quechua, maintaining that the Indians had already been deprived of their dignity, culture, and beliefs and that to finally strip them of their language was to strip them of their identity. The only way to integrate the Indians into Spanish society, Santo Tomás said, was to educate them and do so in their own language. With this in mind, he produced Quechuan grammar texts that he used to teach Quechua to other members of the clergy. Santo Tomás's efforts had far-reaching effects. Quechua was soon picked up and taught in all of the major monasteries in Peru. Thousands of Indians were taught the precepts of Christianity in their own language. They were also taught subjects such as reading, mathematics, and the arts in special schools, which became so well respected that Spanish colonists tried to place their children within them. Within 50 years, Quechua was studied and spoken in Peru and Spain. Even literature was being written in Quechua—by Spanish authors.

Inca Traditions Survive Today

The people of the Andes are resilient. They have overcome the harshest of environments and have withstood conquest and exploitation by Spanish colonists. They have maintained their ancient traditions despite the efforts of the Spanish conquerors to erase their history and culture. In the centuries since Francisco Pizarro conquered the Inca Empire, many Indians have clung to their culture to the point that even at the end of the twentieth century, many descendants of the Incas still do not speak or write Spanish.

The descendants of the Incas have managed to preserve the simple lifestyle of their ancestors. Many are farmers who use the same hillside terraces for crops and the same irrigation canals used by Inca farmers hundreds of years earlier. They live in adobe or stone houses with thatched roofs and interiors that are as spartan and functional as any Inca home in the sixteenth century. Author Ruth Karen writes that the Indians have even revived a form of the Inca *ayllus:* "They move from the highlands to the coast, mostly to the big cities, and there they set up ayllus, communities in which every family has its own house and yard, but all work together for the collective good."[60]

A Peruvian woman sits outside a thatched house similar to Inca homes constructed during the sixteenth century.

Today, some 8 million Quechua and 680,000 Aymara Indians are the direct descendants of the Incas. They form the largest native population in the Western Hemisphere. Many of the Quechua and Aymara live in the highlands of Peru like their ancestors had before them. They still speak Quechua, and despite being outwardly Catholic, they have retained their love and worship of the sun.

Notes

Introduction: The Land of the Incas

1. Pedro de Cieza de León, *The Incas,* trans. Harriet de Onis, ed. Victor Wolfgang von Hagen. Norman: University of Oklahoma Press, 1959, p. 17.

Chapter 1: Ten Thousand Years of Tradition

2. Ruth Karen, *Kingdom of the Sun: The Inca, Empire Builders of the Americas.* New York: Four Winds, 1975, p. 7.

3. James B. Richardson III, *People of the Andes.* Washington, DC: Smithsonian Books, 1994, p. 112.

4. Cieza de León, *The Incas,* p. 283.

5. Quoted in Garcilaso de la Vega, *Royal Commentaries of the Incas and General History of Peru,* part 1. Austin: University of Texas Press, 1966, p. 43.

6. Alfred Métraux, *The History of the Incas.* New York: Pantheon Books, 1969, p. 46.

7. Loren McIntyre, *The Incredible Incas and Their Timeless Land.* Washington, DC: National Geographic Society, 1975, p. 55.

8. John Hemming, *Machu Picchu.* New York: Newsweek Books, 1981, p. 90.

Chapter 2: The Incas

9. Cieza de León, *The Incas,* p. 154.

10. Karen, *Kingdom of the Sun,* p. 78.

11. William H. Prescott, *History of the Conquest of Peru.* New York: Heritage, 1957, pp. 781–82.

12. Michael E. Moseley, *The Incas and Their Ancestors: The Archaeology of Peru.* London: Thames and Hudson, 1992, p. 78.

13. Garcilaso, *Royal Commentaries of the Incas,* part 1, p. 469.

14. Prescott, *History of the Conquest of Peru,* p. 768.

15. Ann Kendall, *Everyday Life of the Incas.* New York: Dorset, 1973, p. 100.

16. Prescott, *History of the Conquest of Peru,* p. 774.

17. Cieza de León, *The Incas,* p. 159.

18. Huamán Poma, *Letter to a King: A Peruvian Chief's Account of Life Under the Incas and Under Spanish Rule,* trans. Christopher Dilke. New York: E. P. Dutton, 1978, p. 87.

19. Cieza de León, *The Incas,* p. 167.

20. Prescott, *History of the Conquest of Peru,* p. 773.

21. Friedrich Katz, *The Ancient American Civilizations,* trans. K. M. Lois Simpson. New York: Praeger, 1972, p. 277.

Chapter 3: Building an Empire

22. Prescott, *History of the Conquest of Peru,* p. 792.

23. Karen, *Kingdom of the Sun,* p. 98.

24. Moseley, *The Incas and Their Ancestors,* p. 53.

25. Sir Clements Markham, *The Incas of Peru.* New York: AMS, 1969, p. 105.

26. Garcilaso, *Royal Commentaries of the Incas,* part 1, p. 31.

27. George Bankes, *Peru Before Pizarro.* Oxford, England: Phaidon, 1977, p. 160.

Chapter 4: Everyone Had a Place in Society

28. Hemming, *Machu Picchu,* p. 92.

29. Karen, *Kingdom of the Sun,* p. 9.

30. Kendall, *Everyday Life of the Incas*, p. 170.

31. Prescott, *History of the Conquest of Peru*, p. 750.

32. Prescott, *History of the Conquest of Peru*, p. 744.

33. Bernabe Cobo, *Inca Religion and Customs*, trans. Roland Hamilton. Austin: University of Texas Press, 1990, p. 194.

34. Garcilaso, *Royal Commentaries of the Incas*, part 1, p. 212.

35. Prescott, *History of the Conquest of Peru*, p. 754.

36. Garcilaso, *Royal Commentaries of the Incas*, part 1, p. 121.

Chapter 5: The Last of the Great Kings

37. Cieza de León, *The Incas*, p. 246.

38. Garcilaso, *Royal Commentaries of the Incas*, part 1, p. 566.

39. Garcilaso, *Royal Commentaries of the Incas*, part 1, p. 566.

40. Garcilaso, *Royal Commentaries of the Incas*, part 1, p. 573.

41. Quoted in Garcilaso, *Royal Commentaries of the Incas*, part 1, p. 577.

42. Philip Ainsworth Means, *Fall of the Inca Empire*. New York: Gordian, 1964, p. 29.

43. Quoted in Agustin de Zárate, *The Discovery and Conquest of Peru*. Middlesex, England: Penguin Books, 1968, pp. 98–99.

Chapter 6: A Historic Encounter

44. Quoted in Prescott, *History of the Conquest of Peru*, p. 938.

45. Jean Descola, *The Conquistadors*. New York: Viking, 1957, p. 271.

46. Prescott, *History of the Conquest of Peru*, p. 952.

47. Hemming, *Machu Picchu*, p. 112.

48. Quoted in Garcilaso, *Royal Commentaries of the Incas*, part 2, p. 707.

49. Métraux, *The History of the Incas*, p. 151.

50. Garcilaso, *Royal Commentaries of the Incas*, part 2, pp. 760–61.

51. Garcilaso, *Royal Commentaries of the Incas*, part 2, p. 804.

52. Hemming, *Machu Picchu*, p. 26

Chapter 7: Life Under Spanish Rule

53. Descola, *The Conquistadors*, p. 293.

54. Garcilaso, *Royal Commentaries of the Incas*, part 2, p. 1440.

55. Garcilaso, *Royal Commentaries of the Incas*, part 2, p. 1481.

56. Means, *Fall of the Inca Empire*, p. 124.

57. Means, *Fall of the Inca Empire*, p. 130.

58. Poma, *Letter to a King*, p. 137.

59. Hemming, *The Conquest of the Incas*, p. 377.

60. Karen, *Kingdom of the Sun*, p. 174.

For Further Reading

John Hemming, *Machu Picchu*. New York: Newsweek Books, 1981. A pictorial history of the discovery and study of the lost Inca city Machu Picchu. It also includes a general history of Peru and a useful appendix.

Friedrich Katz, *The Ancient American Civilizations*. Trans. K. M. Lois Simpson. New York: Praeger, 1972. A comparative history of all of the major native races that have developed in the Americas, including the Aztecs, Incas, and Maya.

Peter Lourie, *Sweat of the Sun, Tears of the Moon: A Chronicle of an Incan Treasure.* New York: Atheneum, 1991. A story of the author's obsessive search for a fabled Inca treasure in Peru.

William H. Prescott, *History of the Conquest of Peru*. New York: Heritage, 1957. One of the seminal histories about the fall of the Inca Empire.

James B. Richardson III, *People of the Andes.* Washington, DC: Smithsonian Books, 1994. A well-written and easy-to-read book about Andes cultures from the first migrant hunter-gatherers to the descendants of the Incas in the modern day. Includes many illustrations, photos, and maps.

Works Consulted

Books

George Bankes, *Peru Before Pizarro.* Oxford, England: Phaidon, 1977. A good general history of the Inca Empire before the conquest by the Spanish.

C. A. Burland, *Peru Under the Incas.* London: George Rainbird Ltd., 1967. Discusses the religious and cultural aspects of life in the Inca empire. He offers detailed descriptions of everyday life and the technologies used in building roads, producing textiles and creating works of art. Includes many black and white photographs and illustrations.

Burr Cartwright Brundage, *Empire of the Inca.* Norman: University of Oklahoma Press, 1963. Brundage presents a history of the Inca empire up to the Spanish conquest, focusing on Inca religion and mythology and their influence on the development of the empire.

Pedro de Cieza de León, *The Incas.* Trans. Harriet de Onis. Ed. Victor Wolfgang von Hagen. Norman: University of Oklahoma Press, 1959. One of the most well regarded chronicles of the Incas from a Spanish soldier who traveled throughout Peru. Although slightly biased by his European world view, his writings are considered to be more objective than most.

Jean Descola, *The Conquistadors.* New York: Viking, 1957. Lively depictions of Spanish conquerors like Cortez and Pizarro and their impact on the indigenous cultures of the New World.

Henry E. Dobyns and Paul L. Doughty, *Peru: A Cultural History.* New York: Oxford University Press, 1976. A history of the cultural evolution of Peru from the first civilizations, including the Inca, to the twentieth century.

Frederic André Engel, *An Ancient World Preserved: Relics and Records of Prehistory in the Andes.* New York: Crown, 1976. A good book about the author's archaeological discoveries with observations about ancient Andes cultures.

Garcilaso de la Vega, *Royal Commentaries of the Incas and General History of Peru,* 2 parts. Austin: University of Texas Press, 1966. The Royal Commentaries offer viewpoints of the conquest from the Spanish and Inca perspectives. Very comprehensive descriptions of Inca history, customs, religion, and politics.

Edward Hyams and George Ordish, *The Last of the Incas: The Rise and Fall of an American Empire.* New York: Simon and Schuster, 1963. The authors present a concise history that covers everything from the succession of Inca rulers to the empire's defeat by the Spanish.

Ruth Karen, *Kingdom of the Sun: The Inca, Empire Builders of the Americas.* New

York: Four Winds, 1975. An easy-to-read and amply illustrated book about Inca culture and customs. Includes some historical fiction in the last few chapters.

Ann Kendall, *Everyday Life of the Incas.* New York: Dorset, 1973. An invaluable resource about the customs and culture of the people who lived in the Inca Empire. Everything from what the Incas ate and drank to their personality traits is covered in detail with illustrations.

Sir Robert Marett, *Peru.* New York: Praeger, 1969. Includes a brief overview of the Incas and the development of Peru after the conquest by the Spanish.

Sir Clements Markham, *The Incas of Peru.* New York: AMS, 1969. Markham was a geographer and explorer who visited Peru. His history is very readable and well regarded by historians.

Loren McIntyre, *The Incredible Incas and Their Timeless Land.* Washington, DC: National Geographic Society, 1975. A general history of the Inca Empire, which includes entertaining personal accounts of the author's travels throughout South America.

Philip Ainsworth Means, *Fall of the Inca Empire.* New York: Gordian, 1964. A summary of the conquest of the Incas and the effects of colonialism on the natives.

Alfred Métraux, *The History of the Incas.* New York: Pantheon Books, 1969. A general history of the Inca Empire with some black and white photographs and illustrations.

Michael E. Moseley, *The Incas and Their Ancestors: The Archaeology of Peru.* London: Thames and Hudson, 1992. A textbook that discusses the Incas and other early Andes cultures in an archaeological context. Includes many illustrations and photographs.

Huamán Poma, *Letter to a King: A Peruvian Chief's Account of Life Under the Incas and Under Spanish Rule.* Trans. Christopher Dilke. New York: E. P. Dutton, 1978. A collection of letters from an Inca chieftain to the king of Spain that details Inca life. Poma describes the harsh treatment of the Indians by the Spanish colonists in an attempt to bring about reform. Illustrated with pen and ink drawings that depict daily life among the Incas.

Agustin de Zárate, *The Discovery and Conquest of Peru.* Middlesex, England: Penguin Books, 1968. Zárate was an eyewitness during the conquest and offers valuable details of events of that period.

Periodicals

John Otis, "Juanita: A Mummy Frozen in Time," *Newsday,* January 9, 1996.

Baird Straughan, "The Secrets of Ancient Tiwanaku Are Benefiting Today's Bolivia," *Smithsonian,* February 1991.

Index

Accllahuaci (the House of
the Chosen Women), 23
administrative system
census and, 35
governors, 29, 49
nobility and, 34
orders of ten, 34–35
origins of, 12
agriculture
described, 41–42
irrigation and, 10, 13, 23
religion and, 36, 39
Almagro, Diego de, 66–67,
70–71, 74
Alvarado, Pedro de, 70
ancestor worship, 36
Andes Mountains, 10
animals, 10
archaeology, 78
architecture
Coricancha, 21–23
of Cuzco, 20, 21, 69
Sacsahuaman, 23–25
of Tiwanaku, 14
army
Inca, 25–27, 28, 73
Spanish, 73
see also warfare
artisans, 43
Atahuallpa (Inca ruler)
division of Inca Empire
and, 57
Spaniards and
captured by, 63–64
defeated by, 73
executed by, 68–69

imprisoned by, 65–66
initial contact with,
61–63
warfare with Huáscar
and, 58–61
Atoc (general), 58, 69
ayllus, 35–36, 47
Aymara (Indians), 81

Bankes, George, 40
Beatriz (Inca princess), 75
Belalcázar, Sebastián de, 70
Bingham, Hiram, 54
burial customs, 37, 38
Burland, C. A., 29

calendars, 23
Cañari (Indians), 58, 59, 76
Capac Ñan, 30–31
Capac Yupanqui (Inca
ruler), 16
caste system, 36–37, 41–44,
45, 46
Cayambi (Indians), 53–54
census, 35
Chaloguchima (general),
58–60
Chanca (Indians), 17, 19
Charles V (Holy Roman
Emperor), 70
Chavín (Indians), 12
chicha, 23, 46
children, 48, 49
Chimu (Indians)
administrative system
of, 12

as artisans, 43
defeat of, 33
irrigation and, 10
Cieza de León, Pedro de
on census, 35
description of Huayna
Capac, 52
on geography of Inca
Empire, 10
on Lake Titicaca, 18
on naming of children, 49
on Pumapumku, 14
on rebuilding of Cuzco,
20–21
on treatment of
conquered peoples, 28
Ciudad de los Reyes, 71
clans, 35–36, 47
clothing, 44, 46–47
Cobo, Bernabe
on chicha, 46
on origins of Incas, 16
Colla (Indians), 17
commoners, 41–42
ancestor worship and,
36
army and, 26
clothing of, 46–47
education of, 48
marriage and, 47
Condorcanqui, José
Gabriel, 80
conquered peoples
religion of, 21, 29, 39
treatment of, 12, 26,
28–30

conquistadores. *See* Spaniards

Coricancha (Enclosure of Gold), 21–23, 37

crime, 44, 48–49

Cusi Huarcay (wife of Sayri), 75

Cuzco, 20–21, 69

Descola, Jean, 74–75

de Soto, Hernando, 61–63

diseases, 56, 79

education
  clergy and, 36
  of commoners, 48
  of nobility, 17, 36, 44–45

emperors, 45
  see also specific emperors

encomienda system, 77–80

Everyday Life of the Incas (Kendall), 42

Ewbanks, Thomas, 78

family life, 47–48

farming
  in Andes, 10
  described, 41–42
  religion and, 36, 39

Felipe, 63

festivals
  agricultural, 36
  baby naming, 49
  food of, 46
  marriage, 47
  religious, 36, 55–56

food, 20, 46

gambling, 42

Garcilaso de la Vega
  on army training, 27
  on Cayambi uprising, 53
  on execution of Tupac, 76
  on medicine, 50–51
  on origin of name *Peru*, 59
  on prophecies, 56–57, 68, 75
  on rebellion of Manco, 72
  on religion, 39
  on Sacsahuaman, 24
  on Spaniards' entrance into Cuzco, 69
  on treatment of babies, 48

gold
  religion and, 21, 43
  Spaniards and, 65–66
  weapons and, 26

governors, 29, 49

Hastu Huallaca (Chanca leader), 17

Hemming, John
  on defeat of Chanca, 19
  on discovery of Machu Picchu, 54
  on *mita* system, 79
  on rebellion of Manco, 72
  on rigidity of caste system, 41
  on slavery, 67

Historia (Cobo), 16

Holy Place, 21

homes, 46

Huacapata (Holy Place), 21

Huamán Poma (Inca chieftain)
  on burial customs, 37
  description of Spaniards by, 57

on *encomienda* system, 79

on punishment for cheating on taxes, 28

Huanca Auqui (general), 60

Huancavelica, 80

Huari (Indians), 10

Huáscar (Inca ruler)
  division of Inca Empire and, 57
  warfare with Atahuallpa, 58–61

Huayna Capac (Inca ruler)
  concubines of, 45
  death of, 57–58
  as emperor, 52
  Spaniards and, 55, 56–57
  uprisings against, 53–55

illnesses, 49–51

Inca by Privilege, 43, 44

Inca Empire
  division of, 57, 58
  extent of, 10, 14
  population of, 12

Inca Roca (Inca ruler), 16–17

Incas
  characteristics of, 41, 46, 65, 67, 69
  current status of, 81
  origins of, 15–16

Incas, The (Cieza de Léon), 18

Incredible Incas and Their Timeless Land, The (McIntyre), 22

inheritance, 36

Inti (god), 23, 39, 40, 45

Inti Raymi (Festival of the Sun), 55–56

Juanita, 38

Karen, Ruth
  on administrators, 34–35
  on agriculture, 42
  on Inca administrative
    system, 12
  on Incas today, 81
  on symbolism of
    rebuilding Cuzco, 21
Kendall, Ann
  on ceremonies before
    battle, 26
  on gambling, 42
  on metalsmithing, 43

Ladrillero, Juan, 18
language, 33, 45, 80–81
legends
  ayllus and, 35–36
  about death, 56
  of origin of Incas, 15–16
  shrines and, 23
  about victory, 17
Letter to a King (Huamán
  Poma), 57
Lima, 71
llamas, 10, 11
Llonque Yupanqui (Inca
  ruler), 15–16
Luque, Fernando, 66–67

Machu Picchu, 54
Machu Picchu (Hemming),
  54
Mama Rahua Occlo
  (mother of Huáscar), 60
Manarí (Indians), 76
Manco Capac, 15, 21
Manco Inca Yupanqui
  (Inca ruler)
  death at Vilcabamba of, 75

as figurehead, 69–70
  rebellion of, 71–73, 75
Marett, Paul, 67
marriage, 45, 47
Mayta Capac (Inca ruler), 16
McIntyre, Loren
  on Coricancha, 22
  on defeat of Chanca, 19
Means, Philip Ainsworth
  on Spanish contact with
    Incas, 61–62
  on treatment of Indians
    by Spaniards, 77
measles, 56
medicine, 49–51
mercury, 80
metalsmithing, 43
Métraux, Alfred
  on Inca acceptance of
    Spaniards, 69
  on myths of Incas, 15
mining, 77, 79–80
mita system, 42–43, 44, 79
Moche (Indians), 13–14
Mochica (Indians), 10
money, 48
Moseley, Michael E., 35–36
myths
  ayllus and, 35–36
  about death, 56
  of origin of Incas, 15–16
  shrines and, 23
  about victory, 17

New Castile, 70
Newsday (newspaper), 38
nobility, 43–45
  administrative system
    and, 34
  ancestor worship and, 36

army and, 26
  clothing of, 44, 46–47
  education of, 17, 36,
    44–45
  religion and, 36–37

omens, 55–57, 61, 68, 75
orders of ten, 34–35
orejones. See nobility
Otis, John, 38

Pachacuti (Inca ruler)
  ancestor worship and, 36
  became emperor, 19
  as military leader, 32
  rebuilding of Cuzco by,
    20–21
  as statesman, 33
  see also Yupanqui
Pasto (Indians), 53
Peru, 59
Peru (Marett), 67
Peru Under the Incas
  (Burland), 29
Pizarro, Francisco
  arrival in Cuzco of, 69
  capture of Atahuallpa
    and, 64
  death of, 74–75
  establishment of Lima
    by, 71
  granted New Castile, 70
  initial contact with Incas,
    61–63
  warfare with Almagro,
    74
Pizarro, Hernando, 70, 71
Pizarro, Juan, 71, 72
Potosí, 79–80
pottery, 13

Prescott, William H.
  on Coricancha, 21, 23
  on greed of Spaniards, 66
  on importance of emperor, 45
  on nobility and crime, 44
  on punishment for crimes, 48–49
  on treatment of conquered peoples, 30
  on victory celebrations, 27–28
  on weapons of Incas, 26
prophecies, 55–57, 61, 68, 75
Pumapumku, 14
Puná (Indians), 54–55
pyramids, 14

Quechua (Indians), 17, 81
Quechua (language), 45, 80
quipus, 28, 33–34, 35
Quizquiz (general), 58–60

religion
  agriculture and, 36, 39
  ancestor worship and, 36
  of Aymara, 81
  beliefs of, 40
  caste system in, 36–37
  Catholic
    encomienda system and, 78–79
    missionaries and, 76
  clergy, 23, 36
  conquered peoples and, 21, 29, 39
  emperors and, 45

festivals of, 36, 55–56
gods, 39–40
gold and, 21, 43
of Quechua, 81
rituals of, 37, 39, 40
sacrifices, 21, 26
shrines, 21–23, 37, 66, 71
Spaniards and, 57, 71
temples of, 21–23
warfare and, 26, 27
see also myths; specific gods
Richardson, James B., III, 13–14
roads, 29, 30–31
Royal Commentaries of the Incas (Garcilaso) 27, 59
Rumiñaui (general), 65, 70

sacrifices, 21, 26, 37, 39
Sacsahuaman, 23–25, 72
Santo Tomás, Domingo de, 80
sapa Incas, 45
  see also specific emperors
Sayri (Inca ruler), 75–76
shrines, 21–23, 37, 66, 71
silver, 65–66
Sinchi Roca (Inca ruler), 15
slavery, 67, 71, 77, 79–80
smallpox, 56
Spaniards
  arrival of, 55
  characteristics of, 67
  greed, 65–68, 69, 77
  described, 57
  entrance into Cuzco of, 69
  Inca prophecies of, 55–57

initial contact with Incas, 61–63
rule of, 77–80

Tahuantinsuyu. See Inca Empire
taxes, 28, 34, 77, 79
Titicaca, Lake, 18
Titu Cusi (Inca ruler), 76
Tiwanaku (Indians), 10, 14
Toledo blade, 73
Toledo, Francisco de, 76–77, 79
Topa Huallpa (Inca ruler), 69
Topa Inca Yupanqui (Inca ruler)
  death of, 52
  defeat of Chimu and, 32–33
  gambling and, 42
trepanning, 51
tribute, 28, 77, 79
Tumibamba, 53
Tupac Amarú (Condorcanqui), 80
Tupac Amarú (Inca ruler), 76–77

Urco (Inca prince), 17

Valverde, Vicente de, 63–64, 68, 70
Vilcabamba, 75, 76, 77
Viracocha (god), 17, 21, 37, 40, 55
Viracocha (Inca ruler), 17, 19

warfare
  army and, 25–26, 27
  against Cayambi, 53

against Chanca, 19
against Chimu, 32, 33
conquered peoples and,
    12, 26, 28–30
between Huáscar and
    Atahuallpa, 58–61
against Puná, 54–55
religion and, 26, 27

against Spaniards
    led by Atahuallpa,
        64–65
    led by Manco, 71–73, 75
    led by Tupac, 76
    led by Tupac Amarú,
        80
    between Spaniards, 74

weapons, 26, 73

Yachahuasi, 17, 44–45
Yahaur Huacac (Inca
    ruler), 17
Yupanqui (Inca prince), 17, 19
    see also Pachacuti (Inca
        ruler)

Picture Credits

About the Author

Dennis Nishi is a freelance writer and graphic designer. He has a degree in English from Long Beach State University in California. His work has been published in several small magazines and newspapers, including the *Long Beach Press Telegram*.